Work Transformed

People, place and purpose

Work Transformed

People, place and purpose

Published by
LID Publishing Limited
The Record Hall, Studio 204,
16-16a Baldwins Gardens,
London EC1N 7RJ, UK

524 Broadway, 11th Floor, Suite 08-120,
New York, NY 10012, US

info@lidpublishing.com
www.lidpublishing.com

A member of:

www.businesspublishersroundtable.com

Printed in Latvia by Jelgavas Tipogrāfij
ISBN: 978-1-911498-63-6

For more information,
E: info@bdg-a-d.com
E: gillparker@bdg-a-d.com
E: colinmacgadie@bdg-a-d.com

BDG architecture + design
East Studio Riverside Walk
Sea Containers
18 Upper Ground
London, SE1 9PD
T: +44 (0)20 7559 7400
E: info@bdg-a-d.com
www.bdg-a-d.com

Content by:
BDG architecture + design

Copy by:
Andy Swann

Photography by:
Adam Childs
Phil Durrant
Gareth Gardner
Phil Hutchinson
Michael Jones
Jefferson Smith
Richard J Wall

Edited by:
Colin Macgadie
Gill Parker
Helen Ieronimo
Andy Swann

Concept by:
Colin Macgadie

Designed by:
BDG

Contents

—

04

Northern Lights

05

Words

06

Credits

Foreword

Cities and their buildings tell us stories. They contain narratives, obvious and hidden, that illuminate their past, their evolution and their purpose. London is fortunate to contain a wealth of the richest stories to be found anywhere in the world. Its layers of history and development - Roman, Saxon, Norman, Tudor - tell tales that began, as in many major cities, with a river.

The Romans settled on the north bank of the Thames nearly 2,000 years ago, where the river narrowed and provided a convenient crossing point to the marshy lands of the south and the straight roads that led to Chichester and Dover. They built a city with walls whose rough brick and stone masonry provided the foundations for the bastions of the medieval city and today these stand proud in open spaces and lie hidden in the basements of modern buildings. They built an amphitheatre, in which gladiators once fought, that now lies beneath the Guildhall Yard, where military bands now play and Livery Masters race with pancakes each Shrove Tuesday. The site of the forum built in Vespasian's time, once a market and meeting place, now houses the Leadenhall Market where bankers and insurers gather to eat, drink and gossip.

The city's walls did not just keep out conquerors or armies but protected the rich merchants and their wealth, as well as the trades that worked there - the apothecaries, goldsmiths, leathersellers, drapers, cordwainers and chandlers. The merchants in the north grew rich as the flood-prone lands across London Bridge became the place

of the poor, the rebellious and the entertaining. A place of culture even when, in the 17th century, theatres like The Globe were built outside the city walls. Those who were not Freemen of the City were charged tolls and taxes to enter through the protected gates or across the famous bridge with its houses, shops and water mills, and its spikes of decapitated criminals. Along the river sprang up wharves and ports: in the 18th century the Pool of London between London and Limehouse was one of the busiest ports in Europe.

The stevedores no longer toil along the South Bank; instead Londoners and tourists stroll along the Thames Path, a planning miracle that has been pieced together, site by site, since its inception in 1948 and now provides an almost uninterrupted pedestrian route from the source of the river to its mouth. It was written into the planning consent for buildings along the Thames that they should provide space for the path. Colonel Richard Seifert, London's busiest architect in the period after World War Two, included it in his designs for a building that was originally planned as a hotel but was converted to offices for the Sea Containers company. The development, including the Doggett's Coat and Badge pub and a block of apartments, was completed in the 1980s.

Today, the building has been repurposed. A hotel has been reinserted into the structure and the rest designed to house the offices of the Ogilvy & Mather advertising agency. The tourists mix with workers as they make their way to the building and follow routes through the retro-fitted offices that tell narratives of their own - the exposed structures reveal the story of the original construction, voids cut through the concrete waffles tell of the stone and steel from which the structure is made. Movement through and up the building is designed to maximize the impact of views of the river, while the open spaces reflect the democratisation of the workplace and the agility and flexibility that the wireless era permits. The rooftop, which was once the inaccessible territory of the heating and cooling plant, now houses a garden with spectacular views across the capital. It tells us of the need for more efficient use of land in a crowded and growing city, of the importance of wellbeing in the modern workplace, of biodiversity and the enduring fascination of the city skyline. Those views inspired the Italian painter Canaletto in the 1740s and 1750s when Sir Christopher Wren's church spires dominated the river view. Today, the cluster of nicknamed office towers - the Gherkin, the Cheesegrater, the Scalpel, the Walkie Talkie and the Shard - has created photo opportunities that balance the more traditional views of St Paul's, Westminster Abbey and Buckingham Palace with an image of a modern, 21st century city.

This rich mix of old and new is a part of London's story. Its history of fires and bombing has allowed the city to refresh itself while holding onto key buildings. The Great Fire in 1666 allowed London to be rebuilt with modern, fire-resistant buildings that created the governing centre from which Britain would rule over half the globe. The fact that it was built on a medieval street plan maintained the tight nucleus of streets that creates its character today. South of the river, the Festival of Britain, built on sites cleared by the Blitz in World War Two, began the process whereby historic cultural and entertainment activities returned to the area.

Warehouses were converted into museums, galleries and studios. The Bankside Power station became the Tate Modern gallery. So it continues. Seifert's Sea Containers has a new lease of life, its spaces reconfigured for the modern age. This reworking of London's heritage preserves many of the stories that the buildings embody and contain, and adds layers of richness to the architecture and its surroundings. Visible narratives of creativity and entertainment in contexts of past exclusion contribute to a robust identity that enhances London's attractiveness as a place for business in the 21st century.

Peter Murray
Chairman, New London Architecture

We are a team of architects,
designers and creative thinkers.

We are listeners and
communicators, collaborators
and solution seekers.

We believe that architecture is
most successful when it is able
to connect people and spaces.

Our role is to help make those
connections. That's why we focus
on finding the unique solution
for each client.

Every transformation has a story,
unique to the business, its people
and their space.

01

Life by the Sea

-

Stories about moving home

Humans have always gravitated to the water's edge. Water itself helps us survive and thrive, and over the years the banks of waterways like the mighty Thames have attracted people to travel and to trade. The South Bank is no exception – a place of learning and exchange, where ideas are created, plans are made and the possibility of the city is laid out for all to see, on a meandering course that flows towards the mighty ocean. Here can be found many iconic buildings, from Shakespeare's Globe and the Tate Modern, to the severe angles of the National Theatre. Between them all sits Sea Containers. A fixture of the area, it's a building that had lost its way. Now found again, its rejuvenated guise is once more attracting people to the South Bank, as a place where they belong.

——

A hop, skip and a jump

With limited time and
money available for
relocation, BDG moved
to a new space on the
opposite side of the
Thames, inheriting
a concrete shell and
creating a studio
environment that
doubles as a study
in raw simplicity.

A room with a view

Among the brutal
architecture and river
views of the South Bank
is a long-established
creative community that
has grown organically
over the last 40 years;
it was the ideal place for
global media agency MEC
to make its home.

The curious,
the courageous and
the generous

Situated along London's
'Creative Mile' on the
South Bank, surrounded
by leading arts and
cultural establishments,
commanding one of the
most inspiring views
of London old and new,
the new headquarters
for Ogilvy Group UK was
an opportunity to fuse
creative culture and
working space.

The sky's the limit

The best views and
some of the best food,
drink and hospitality on
the South Bank create
a truly exceptional
environment for the
2,300 people working
at Sea Containers.

A hop, skip and a jump

—

Preface:
With limited time and money available for relocation, BDG moved to a new space on the opposite side of the Thames, inheriting a concrete shell and creating a studio environment that doubles as a study in raw simplicity.

01

01
In progress
fit-out of the
interconnecting
stair from ground
to first floor.

02
The BDG studio, with
non hierarchical and
flexible workbench.

03
Much of the
original concrete
and steel structure
was left exposed
and carrying the
scars of previous
construction work.

03

04

London's cultural showpiece is defined by unique and cutting-edge architecture; a landmark location next to the Thames where people flock for drama, art and enjoyment. From around the world, they come here to laugh, to look, to wonder and to talk. The South Bank isn't a location, it's a destination, a riverside community inhabited by the most creative performers and visited by the broadest audience.

The corner of one of its most iconic buildings lay unused and unloved, carrying the scars of neglected years and inconsistent use. It was an eyesore for some, but for the creative it was a blank canvas to work their magic. BDG's growing team of architects, designers and creative thinkers was in need of a new home, a place to really make its own – somewhere it could perform every single day. The result was that people and place grew together to form a bond.

Transforming the cavernous space, full of rigid angles where concrete meets steel, was an opportunity to show the world what was possible. The aim was to create an inspirational home for the future, while keeping the essence of what it means to be BDG. The timescale was tight, but the challenge to write a new chapter together was an exciting one.

The team created a studio that is at once showpiece and clubhouse. Defining our identity, it's a place of pride – a location from which to practice what we preach. We have been able to achieve flexible working in an inspirational setting that is well-connected and comfortable, social and collaborative, with the space to think. It's not a workplace in the traditional sense; it's where we congregate to create. It's where we belong. Physically it's no more than a hop, skip and a jump from our last home, but it's a huge leap in every other way.

04
Unearthed graffiti
within the original
waffle slab ceiling.

05
The integrated
kitchen and
workshop,
positioned at the
heart of the space.

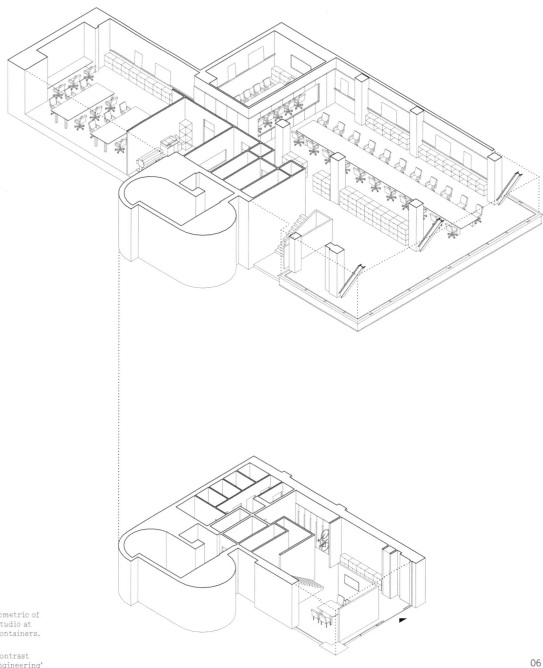

06
Axonometric of
BDG studio at
Sea Containers.

07
The contrast
of 'engineering'
between the
building fabric
and the workplace
solutions.

08
Agility and
communication sit
at the heart of the
BDG culture, with
both practised
around the primary
workbench setting.

06

The Facts:

Size: 400sqm
Location: London
Status: Completed
Year: 2014

Key Features:

Existing and exposed
waffle slab concrete
ceiling above bespoke,
oversized cantilevered
workbench by Knoll.

Opinion:

Published, USM Haller
50 Years of Design and
Innovation, 2015

Published, Make it Yours!
Edition No.1, 2016

07

08

09
Architects,
designers and
strategists co-exist
through integrated
project teams
supported by
the studio
creative wall of
current work.

10
Informal meeting
space on the
river lounge.

11
River view
overlooking
Blackfriars Bridge.

09

10

11

Across the river, the bright lights of the West End beckon with their promise of excitement. The wide windows of this building capture the energy of London's heartland and succeed in channelling the excitement to the environment within.

MEC is bold and it needed a bold workplace to match. A unique, outspoken and energetic brand that makes waves for its clients, it's no surprise that it made its home here. It's a natural fit.

The challenge was clear. Take a space in the heart of a co-located building, nestled among peers, and retain individual identity. Harness the benefits of collaboration, idea-sharing and alternative perspectives, without losing the personality that makes MEC unique. Be bold, be brave, be energized, be the living, breathing manifestation of the view defined by those windows.

MEC's new workplace retains its dynamic personality, radiating its identity and unleashing people to work in new and flexible ways. Designed to inspire, it's a place for its own people. To be creative and to thrive, you need to be present and connected. This space is all of those things. Just look outside.

A room with a view

—

Preface:
Among the brutal architecture and river views of the South Bank in London is a long-established creative community that has grown organically over the last 40 years, the ideal place for global media agency MEC to make its home.

01

02

01
Arrival at MEC
on Level 07 at
Sea Containers.

02
Agile workspace
and integrated
IT solutions allow
staff to choose
where to work.

03
Interconnecting
cast in-situ
concrete stair
between Levels
06 and 08.

03

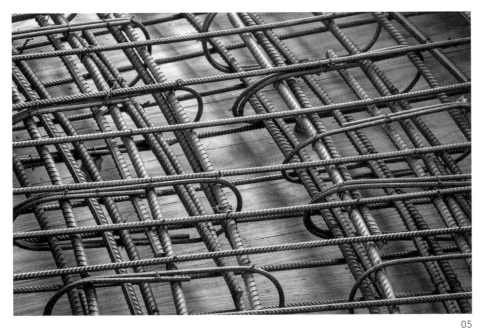

04
Only the second
of its kind in the
UK when built, the
concrete helical
stair cantilevers
within the new
void between
Levels 06 and 08.

05-06
In progress
shots of the
reinforcement
and temporary
supports.

05

06

07

07
Detail of steel and mesh balustrade / handrail integration with concrete stair.

08
The stair sits at the heart of communication between the three floors MEC occupies within Sea Containers.

09
The geometry of the stair is carefully calibrated to allow ease of use for multiple people and fit seamlessly into the existing structural grid.

10
Hard concrete, timber and glass surfaces are offset with coloured fabric acoustic panels.

09

11

12

13

14

15

16

11-12, 14-17
A selection of completed
work with Creative
Agency Acrylicize.

13
In situ cast
interconnecting concrete
stair, one of only two
in the UK at the time
of completion.

17

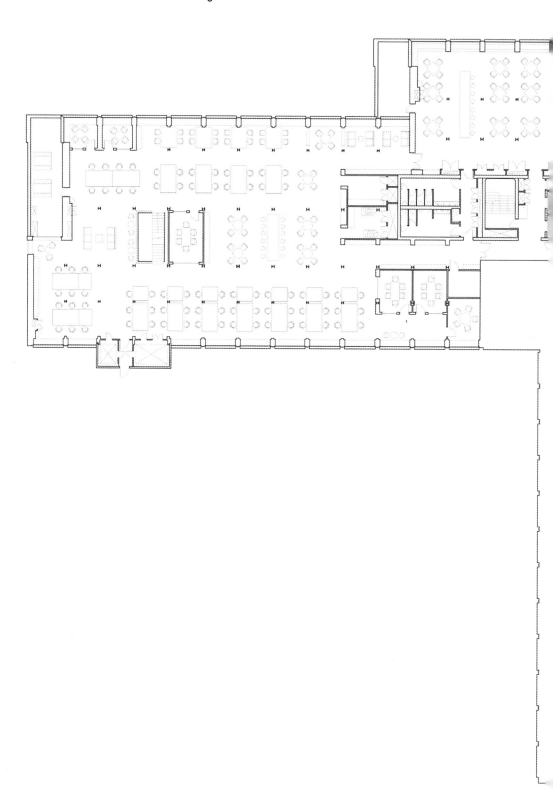

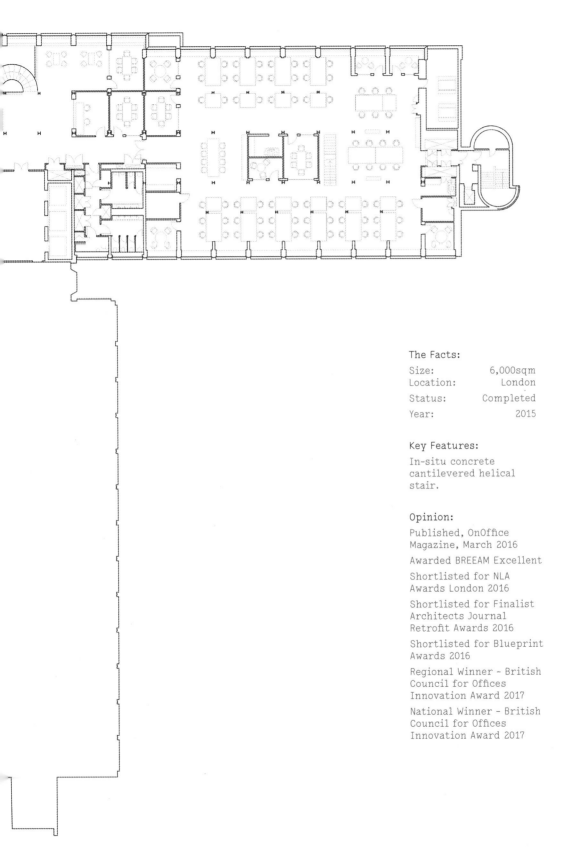

The Facts:

Size:	6,000sqm
Location:	London
Status:	Completed
Year:	2015

Key Features:

In-situ concrete
cantilevered helical
stair.

Opinion:

Published, OnOffice
Magazine, March 2016

Awarded BREEAM Excellent

Shortlisted for NLA
Awards London 2016

Shortlisted for Finalist
Architects Journal
Retrofit Awards 2016

Shortlisted for Blueprint
Awards 2016

Regional Winner - British
Council for Offices
Innovation Award 2017

National Winner - British
Council for Offices
Innovation Award 2017

The curious,
the courageous
and the generous

—

Preface:
Situated along London's 'Creative Mile' on the
South Bank, surrounded by leading arts and
cultural establishments, commanding one of
the most inspiring views of London old and new,
the new headquarters for Ogilvy Group UK was
an opportunity to fuse creative culture and
working space.

01
External photo of
Sea Containers.
Copyright The
Mondrian Hotel.

02
Approximately 50%
of the building
was inherited
'shell and core'.

03
Informal,
co-working space
was located along
the river elevation.

04
The existing
structure, visible
from Riverside
Walk, was re-lined
to complement
the large-scale
structural icons
along the
South Bank.

02   03

True creativity comes from exploration – when we unlock the shackles of the structures our brain uses to understand the world as we know it and dive head first into adventure. There's so much to experience in the world, so why do so many of us work in confined boxes where rigid, standardized shapes define what we recognize as a workplace and, as a result, our brains do only what they recognize as 'work'?

Coming in every day should be an exciting adventure that promises the freedom to explore and experience, meet people, see new things. Imagine if you could define your own path, in a building where your work and its setting offered an unlimited number of possibilities. Imagine how good your work would be if you were handed the power to create your own experience and match it to your exact mood, requirement or notion. Imagine if your daily journey through your workplace threw in a range of stimuli from unexpected conversations and collaborations, new tastes, sprawling views above a city, only metres from tourists who part with hard-earned cash for the same privilege. Imagine the possibilities in a workplace designed for interaction, where every floor offers new experiences. An unexpected event or performance, some quiet space, a huge window, a ledge to perch on, a corner to think, a passing smile, artwork, tasty food or

04

a great coffee. Imagine if your working day was fuel for your mind, body and soul, where you could leave at the end invigorated and inspired, not broken and exhausted.

That's exactly what Sea Containers is. A workplace where people choose to stay and socialize, one where day seamlessly turns to night and, no matter the time, there's an opportunity to work, to think, to rest, to play, to be yourself. Everyone talks about work-life balance, but on one level the equation is simple. Take the dilapidated shell of a once-great building in a bold location and make a statement with it. Be brave enough to cut away floor plates and make dramatic changes to what constitutes a workplace. Design a place for the people who will use it every day, not in spite of them. Create spaces instead of formal offices. Create opportunity where normally workers find monotony. If your people thrive and are out there doing their best work, your company will thrive too.

This building delivers all that and more.

Sea Containers has a personality that's literally built in and it gifts positivity and inspiration to all who inhabit it.

05   06

07

08

05
Interventions were
carefully placed to
expose the original
fabric of the building.

06
Staff can choose
where they want to
work, including prime
space overlooking
the river.

07
Senior leaders sit
open plan within
the business.

08
Formal, informal,
traditional,
collaborative –
the landscape
for co-working
is tailored to
the needs of
the business.

The Facts:
Size: 14,000sqm
Location: London
Status: Completed
Year: 2015

Key Features:
Generous floor to ceiling
heights and the exposed
concrete and steel
structure provide the
setting for an ambitious
flexible working
environment.

Opinion:
Published, OnOffice
Magazine, March 2016

Awarded BREEAM Excellent

Shortlisted for NLA Awards
London 2016

Shortlisted for Finalist
Architects Journal Retrofit
Awards 2016

Shortlisted for Blueprint
Awards 2016

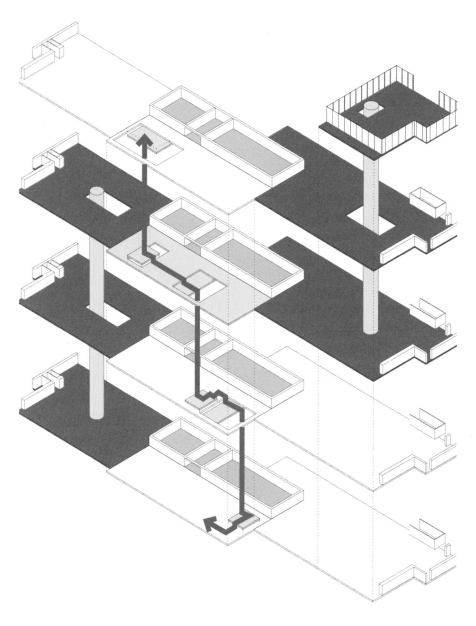

9

09
Conceptual diagram
to illustrate
communication and
interconnectivity
between levels.

10-11
The central
terrace provides
a multitude of
worksettings for
both individual
and collaborative
working.

12
Every space is
designed to be
utilized, including
the concrete
platforms under
the stairs.

13
Structural
interventions
open up the space
to create both
double and triple
height voids.

10

11

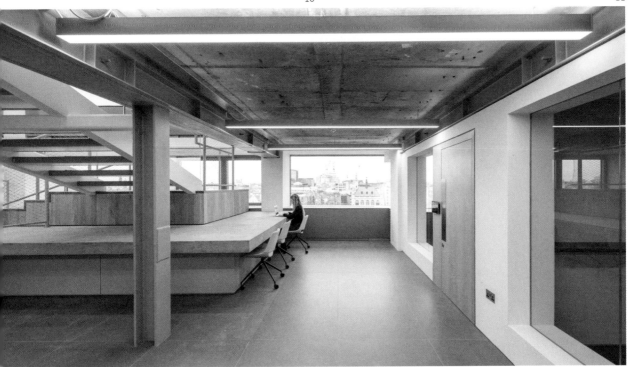

12

13

14

14-15
Competition
winning
visualisations.

16-17
Stage 3 developed
design working
model.

15

16

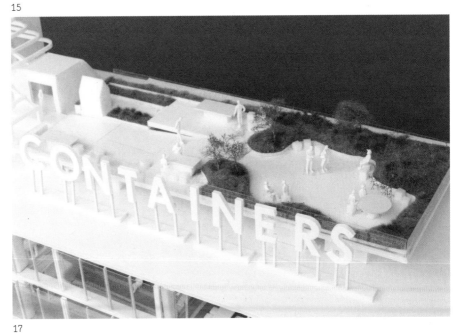

17

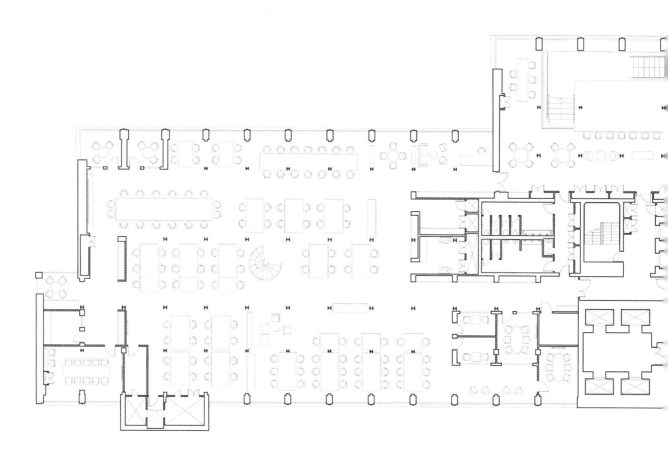

19

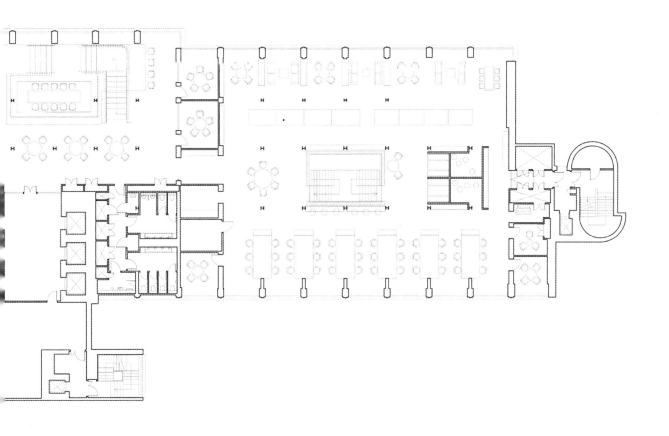

18
Interconnectivity
betweenLevels 09 and 11
within the central
terrace.

19
Level 10 loose
furniture general
arrangement.

20

20
Ogilvy Group UK
informal
meeting space.

21
The central
terrace Level 09 to 11
co-working space.

22-23
Alternative
worksettings
are distributed
throughout the
space to support
the requirements
of the business.

24
The 'Heart of Glass'
meeting room on
Level 09, visibly
integrated within
the agency.

21

22

23

"Without a doubt, one of the finest, most creative working environments created in recent times."

—

George Roberts
Partner | London Markets
Head of Client Strategy
Cushman & Wakefield

The sky's the limit

■

Preface:

The best views and some of the best
food, drink and hospitality on the
South Bank create a truly exceptional
environment for the 2,300 people
working at Sea Containers.

01

Gaze out through panoramic glass from a vantage point that offers distant glimpses of the countryside beyond the city, or head up to the rooftop deck for a 360-degree view across the bustling capital prove that this place to eat, drink and relax is a destination within a destination.

People are encouraged to flow through the building, journeying upwards through the levels to reach this pinnacle. The serenity of the interior is matched only by the dynamic view of the city outside. It provides not just a superior work experience but provides spaces to entertain clients or simply unwind after a busy day.

From the hustle and bustle of eating areas, with food stalls and pop-ups, to the quieter corners of remote working areas, to the vibrancy of the bars, as teams come together to reflect on the day's achievements, this space offers choice and opportunity, whatever the occasion.

Choose the tranquillity of the Cucumber Bar for a restaurant and cocktail experience, with its fine coffee and thoughtful menus. Share the view with clients on the balcony, or take a window table and gaze over London as you dine. For an important meeting, the private dining area creates the optimum productivity and hospitality experience.

Wander slowly towards the auditorium, while taking in the stunning city skyline, as the multi-level, multi-use space opens out in front of you, or head toward the welcoming glow of the Sunset Bar.

There is a private members' club for everyone who works here – this is their exclusive network, a place to belong.

01
External terrace in the Cucumber Bistro, Level 13.
02
The Cucumber Bar, offering a host of bespoke cocktails, craft beer and wine.

02

03

05

04

03-04
The Sunset Bar
on Level 13 detailed
in stainless steel
and Pyrolave finishes.

05
The infrastructure
within the
building allows
for connected
working anywhere,
including in the
external spaces
looking over the
city skyline.

06
Client facing
conference suite
on Level 12, with
flexible spaces
to accommodate
a full range
of meetings.

06

07

08

09

10

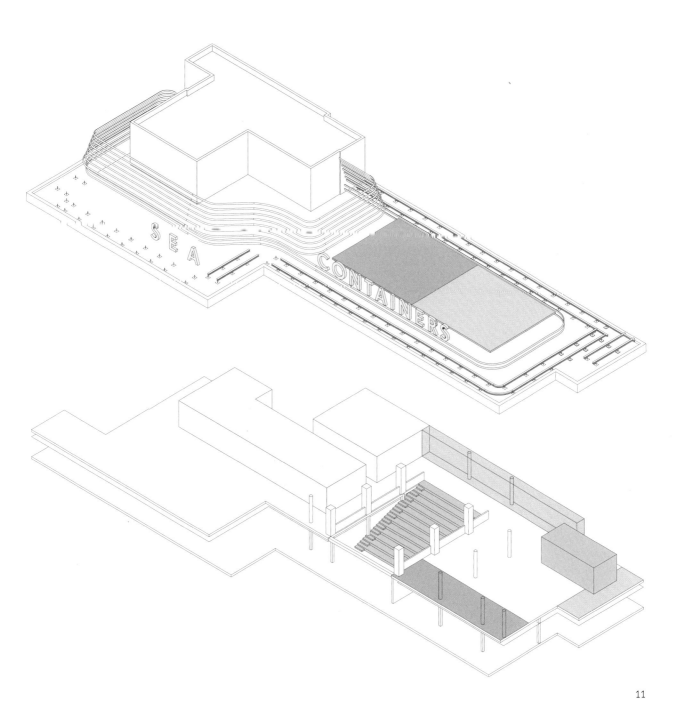

07
The stunning Level
12-13 amphitheatre,
overlooking the river.

08-10
Ladyhawke launches
her new album at
Sea Containers.

11
Diagram showing
Stage 3 developed
design programme
for the Sky Terrace
at Sea Containers.

The Facts:

Size:	2,100sqm
Location:	London
Status:	Completed
Year:	2015

Key Features:
Bespoke hospitality
settings that provide
incredible social spaces
as well as areas to
work with the benefit
of unparalleled views
over London.

Opinion:
Published, OnOffice
Magazine, March 2016

Published, Wallpaper,
March 2016

Published, OnOffice
Magazine, September 2016

Published, MIX
Interiors, September 2016

Published, Office
Snapshots, September 2016

Published, Archdaily,
October 2016

Published, FX Magazine,
October 2016

Published, MIX
Interiors, October 2016

Published, Design
Insider, November 2016

Published, Detail,
November 2016

Published, The Times,
December 2016

Awarded BREEAM Excellent

Shortlisted for NLA Awards
London 2016

Shortlisted for Finalist
Architects Journal Retrofit
Awards 2016

Shortlisted for
Blueprint Awards 2016

13

12

12
Carefully crafted
access to the
rooftop terrace
within the existing
plant enclosure for
the building.

13
The rooftop terrace.
A space that sits
among the London
skyline and the
iconic signage for
the building.

02
Out of Office

-

Giving life back to the city

We live in the age of 'always on'.
The relentless pace of the world
means work integrates into our
lives in different ways. Gone are
the days when the whistle blows
at five and office workers stream
into the late afternoon as a single
exodus out towards the suburbs. We
are now global and connected, and
we work in new ways. To support
that, we need a different kind of
workplace. The lines are blurred
between work and life; it's no
longer a question of balance, but of
integration. If we're able to work
at home, we need to feel at home at
work. Productive places that help
us to work, rest and play in any
way we choose, at any time, are
not a thing of the future. They are
already breathing new life not only
into our relationship with work,
but into the cities they inhabit.

Creative regeneration

—

Preface:

As one of the largest shipping ports in Europe, Hamburg has long been established as a leading transport hub, but as WPP co-locates its agencies and media companies into a new city centre workspace, it also hopes to establish the city as a creative hub.

01

02

03

01
View of internal
covered courtyard
and main reception.

02
Historical photo
of the interior
of Zeise Halle.

03
Ground floor
conference room.

04

04
Ground floor cafe space
programmed to be open to
the street and accessed by
the public.
05-07
BDG work in progress
to develop the design
and provide briefing
for the developer to
deliver the full
solution, fit for the
client, from the
outside in.

Even today, as media and
financial institutions
find their place in
its former industrial
buildings, Hamburg acts
as a hub – connecting
people, places and
activity. Journeys,
movement from one
place to another, are
part of its very fabric,
so it's no surprise to
discover the old and the
new colliding here.

In a place famous for
shipping, with an
industrial heritage still
visible in the facades of
its buildings, a group
of the most modern
agencies and media
companies decided to
take a journey together
and create a hub of their
own. Congregating as one
in a single location,

yet remaining as
individual as they ever
were, this represents
a transition unlike so
many that Hamburg has
seen, yet it remains
in keeping with the
traditions of the city.

Co-location leads to
collaboration and co-
creation. There are more
measurable business
drivers, but these are
the things that make the
greatest impact. Bringing
these people together
in an inspirational
setting allows them to
work in new and exciting
ways and creates new
journeys for individuals,
companies, groups and
clients. It's a transition
from the present to the
future, with one eye on
the past.

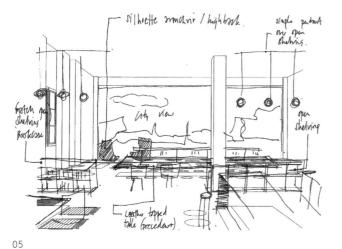

05

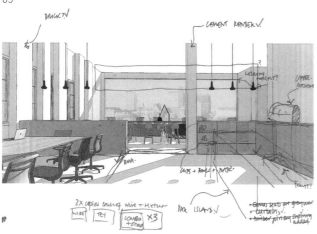

06

The Facts:
Size: 14,000sqm
Location: Hamburg
Status: On-site
Year: 2017

Key Features:
A facade designed to integrate with the local street scape – one building within that looks like a collection of different buildings from the outside.

Opinion:
Shortlisted for DGNB Gold
Shortlisted for UK 2017 Project at FX Awards

07

01

02

01
Newly installed rooflights
within the external terrace
bring light to both ground
and lower ground floor
studio space.
02
The arrival to the studio
shuns the traditional
reception in favour of
an open meeting space.
03
The 'cube' meeting room
connects arrival with
the studio space on
ground floor.

03

The ideas factory

—

Preface:

Situated in what was historically
an area of breweries, workshops
and factories, Brewhouse Yard in
Clerkenwell, London is now at the
centre of a creative community
that has been further enhanced by
the arrival of an award winning
studio space for global design
agency Brand Union.

The angles and lines echo days past when brewers concocted new and exciting infusions alongside their old classics. Teams in which everyone played their part in creating something to be shared and sampled around the world once walked these floors. Today they do so again. There's a heritage of creation in this part of London.

This has always been a creative place for creative people, but today that reality has been taken to a new level. The addition of playfulness and freedom where once there was process, casts light into the deepest recesses of the basement – a place where teams huddle to plan and plot. Deliberate hiding places for quiet thinking and conversation blend seamlessly into corners, while an amphitheatre spans the divide between floors. Hewn from the thick concrete slab, the marks of the industrial cutters

that made this new incarnation possible are there to see and to touch.

For a company whose website leads with the statement 'Brilliantly Designed, Beautifully Connected', there was no alternative. This space had to be perfect and give a stunning local identity to the UK arm of this global community.

Meander through the levels of the building where modern connected technology gives an unrestricted freedom to work, seamlessly integrating with exposed brickwork, steel frames and durable, industrial staircases. Experience the inspiration that comes from being present in this workplace, hidden in the creative heart of London.

There's always another corner to turn, another space to explore, another way to work. This is the place where curiosity fuels the imagination.

04

04
The 'Factory' contains a workshop and integrated storage for staff.

05
Installations within the double height studio space on ground floor - housing a host of non-bookable collaborative settings for varying size teams and activities.

06
The ground floor studio accommodates the UK Brand Union agency, as well as the global leadership team - separated by the factory themed glazing, but visible to all.

05

06

07

08

10

09

07
Terrace seating provides a space for meetings and events, as well as connecting the ground floor studio with the lower ground.

08
The studio was designed with a deliberate domestic scale within the industrial space.

09
Creative workspace, personally branded by the studio.

10
Impromptu meetings within reception showcases the creative nature of the studio to visitors upon arrival.

11
General arrangement of the ground floor studio at Brewhouse Yard.

11

The Facts:

Size:	3,000sqm
Location:	London
Status:	Completed
Year:	2014

Key Features:

A facade designed to integrate with the local streetscape - one building within that looks like a collection of different buildings from the outside.

Opinion:

Published, FM Magazine, December 2015

Published, Mix Interiors, May 2015

Winner BCO Award 2015, Fit Out of Workplace London and South East

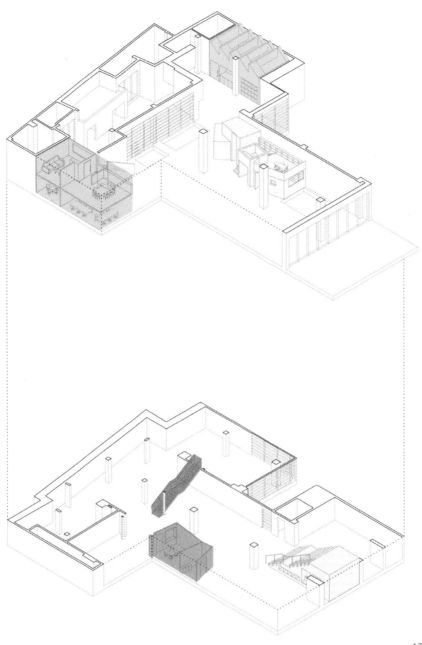

13

12
The studio
arrival and
reception
space on
the ground
floor.

13
Diagram
showing the key
interventions
within the
ground and
lower ground.

14
Concrete - brick
- block, detailing
was key to
connecting the
existing fabric
of the building
with the new.

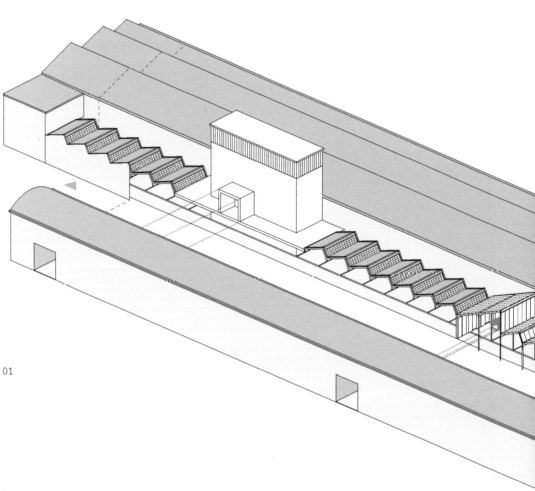

01

01
Diagram showing
the new glazed
link and core
arrangement to
unify the existing
factory buildings.

Taking the
long view

—

Preface:
In Milan, a global hub for fashion, culture and design, a group of leading creative agencies aims to redevelop a collection of low-rise and neglected industrial buildings with a canal-facing frontage of over 200 metres, establishing a new centre of excellence for the future.

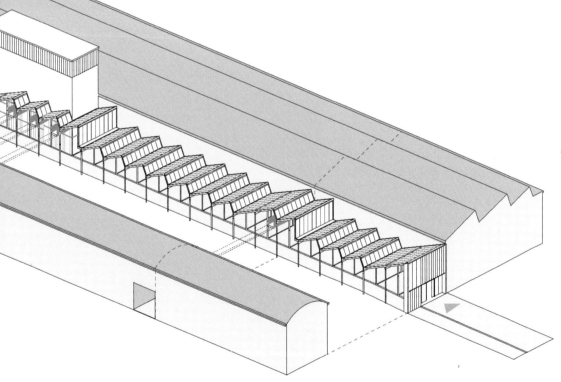

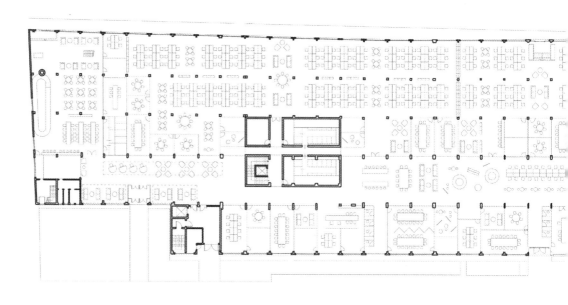

A global epicentre of the most refined in fashion, culture and design, Milan is a place where appearance matters almost as much as function. On its catwalks, tomorrow's fashions are showcased today. Prominent and visual, every step taken on them is part of an elaborate parade that demands attention.

Think of this building as a catwalk. A long, narrow walkway that faces its audience in the city, passing by on and around the adjacent waters. On it and in it, creative people parade their talents, launching ideas to the world to rapturous applause. Individuals, collectives, teams and collaborators, the only limits these people face are those of their imagination.

How to take buildings that represent this dream in shape and make them everything they need to be in spirit? To forge a beating heart of creativity and create a place that acts as a genuine showcase of the future from a context of rundown neglect is no simple task.

By staying true to the heritage of Milan, and of the buildings themselves, a simple, refined and dynamic creation turns old to new.

With the right creative input, neglected becomes the new chic.

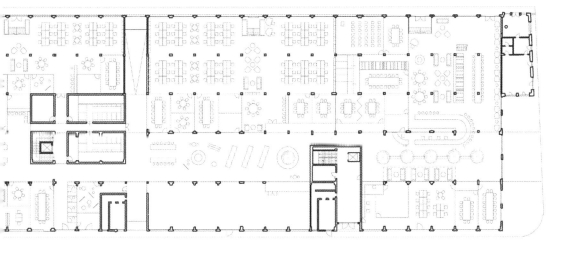

02

03

04

02
Ground floor
general
arrangement
furniture plan.

03
The original
factory building
facing the canal.

04
Large spaces
with great
natural daylight
from the
existing north
rooflights will
make exceptional
studio space for
the creative
business relocating
in 2018.

The Facts:
Size: 16,800sqm
Location: Milan
Status: In progress
Year: 2018

Key Features:
Retained interior spaces
opening out onto a new
glazed link / atrium
between the two
existing buildings.

Opinion:
-

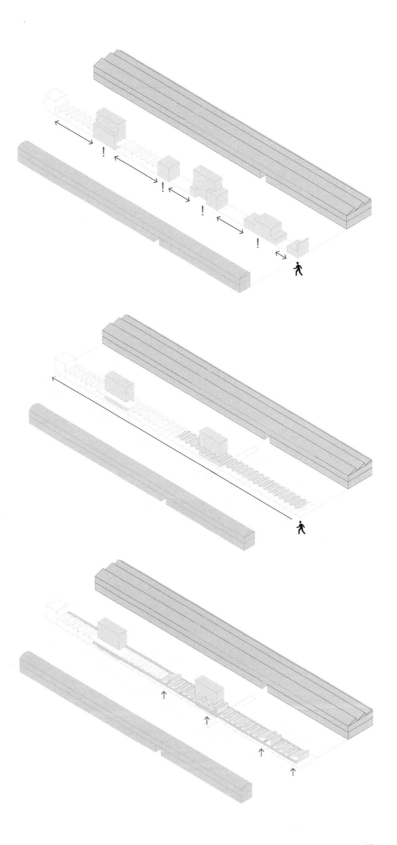

05
A series of
diagrams that
identify the
transformation
from the existing
nature / condition
of the link
between the two
buildings, to the
new rationalized
programme.
06-07
Visualisations of
both the external
and internal vision
for the new link.

05

01

Down by the waterfront

02

03

Preface:
Portugal's capital enjoys plenty of sunshine
and a celebrated cultural scene. Among a host
of plans for regeneration across the city is the
refurbishment of a long-derelict building on the
waterfront that houses a media centre for some
of the city's leading agencies.

Lisbon's waterfront is the perfect place to gaze back at a city of contrasts and togetherness, where differences create wonder. A settlement built on hills, where ancient meets modern and traditional crafts blend seamlessly with cutting-edge commerce. The waterfront itself gives the opportunity for productive relaxation – behind you, the inspiring city rises with its own architectural identity, while before you the Atlantic Ocean opens out onto the world.

In a renaissance city, a derelict building is something to be treasured, and represents a chance to bring together tradition with modern drive. Rescuing and re-purposing such a building as a dynamic media centre, where thriving creative agencies amalgamate and congregate to bring their work to life, is the essence of Lisbon.

Remaining sympathetic to the building's heritage in its enviable waterside setting is essential, but just as important is the demand to create a connected, creative workplace that's fit for the future. Creating this kind of space takes a deft touch, using the story of the building and its surroundings to inspire its future.

This new incarnation isn't a question of tearing down the old to replace it with the new; it's the writing of a new chapter in the building's history.

Staying in contact with the traditions of the building, offering glimpses into its past while creating new, exciting spaces within its structure, is just the start. Connecting with the city and the sea outside, capturing and catalysing, creates a place for the people who will be creating within it. Like Lisbon itself, the future of this building is lively yet laid back, and most important of all, lacking in pretence.

04

The Facts:
Size: 8,000sqm
Location: Lisbon
Status: On-site
Year: 2017

Key Features:
Large open workspaces,
with generous floor to
ceiling heights and
expansive views over
the harbour.

Opinion:
-

05

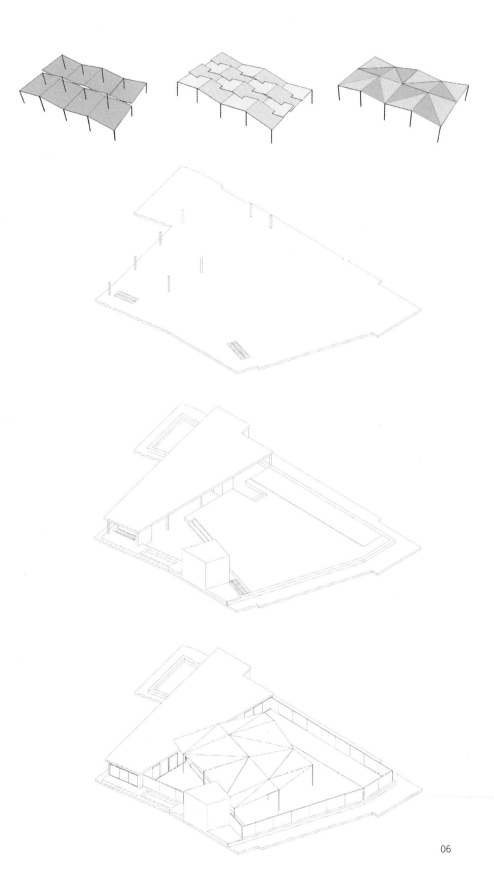

01-03
Photographs
of the
existing site.

04-06
Concept design
materials for
the rooftop
terrace and
business lounge.

06

A new lease of life

—

Preface:
A 35,000sqm unused and redundant building in the heart of Madrid provides the setting for full scale redevelopment and the creation of a new urban campus, designed to reinvigorate the neighbourhood and the businesses that take up residency.

02

03

01

04

05

Bustling, energetic, vibrant, Madrid pulses with energy like only a capital city can. Acting as Spain's gateway to the world, it also provides a window to its culture. Community and family come first – every individual is part of something bigger than themselves.

So it is with this new urban campus. The neglect of a huge and cavernous building has left a hole in the centre of its community. Once again, it's ready to rise as a beacon of Madrid's famous 24-hour lifestyle. A coming together of individual creative agencies, bonded as family through WPP, ready to inject life into the building with new and exciting purpose.

Transforming such a colossus into a modern workplace is one challenge. Purposing it to contribute positively to the community, both inside and outside its walls, is another entirely. It's a place that will be owned by individual operating companies, by the group they belong to, by the locality it inhabits and by Madrid as a whole.

The facade of the building offers the chance to make it such a focal point. A place that brings people together as they naturally flow. Individually and collectively, communities form and are forged, just as traditional identities are retained. The building unlocks all of this, with brave yet sensitive design, carefully planned for all of these people.

From the heart of the city, this place reflects everything that makes Madrid.

06

07

01-04
Photos of the
existing building
at 26 Rios Rosas
- previously
occupied by
Telefonica.

05
The remains of
the previous
occupiers fit-out
awaiting removal.

06-07
The building
laid bare
and awaiting
structural
alteration
ahead of fit-out.

08
Conceptual diagrams
exploring variation
and openness for
the new facade as
a contrast to
existing condition.

09
The introduction
of a layered
approach to the
facade to highlight
the verticality of
the design and
transparency of
the building to
the city.

10
Stage 3
visualisation of
the proposed
North facing
facade on
Rios Rosas.

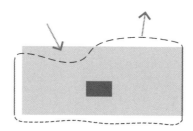

08

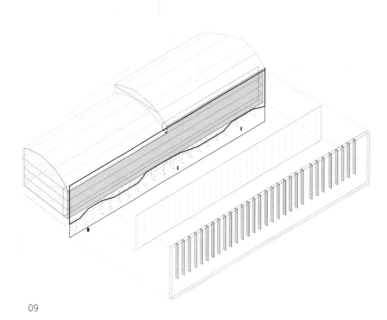

09

10

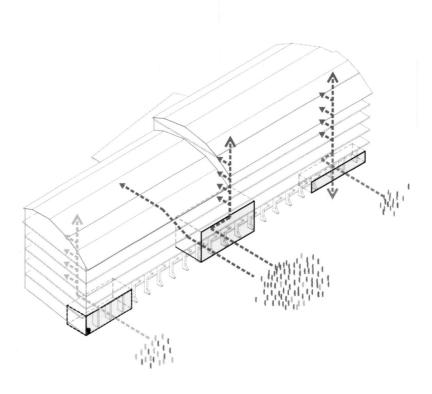

11

11
Definition of
access to the
building through
introduction of
a new central
entrance and
primary core.
12
Stage 3
visualisation of
the new entrance
from Rios Rosas.
13
Stage 3
visualisation of
the new reception.

12

13

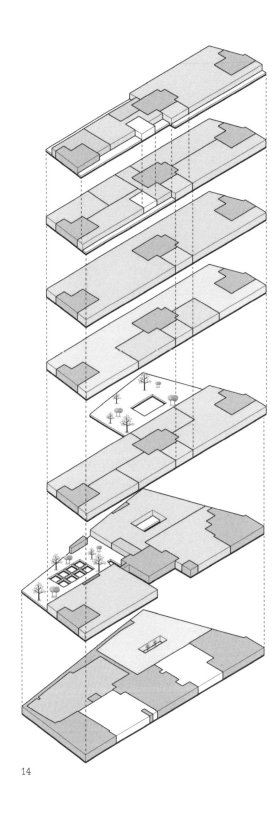

14

15

14
The programme
for the 'Hybrid'
building, which
mixes use classes
and activity to
redefine the
notion of a 9 to 5
office building.

15
Stage 2 concept
visualisation
highlighting
the variety of
large settings
within the overall
programme.

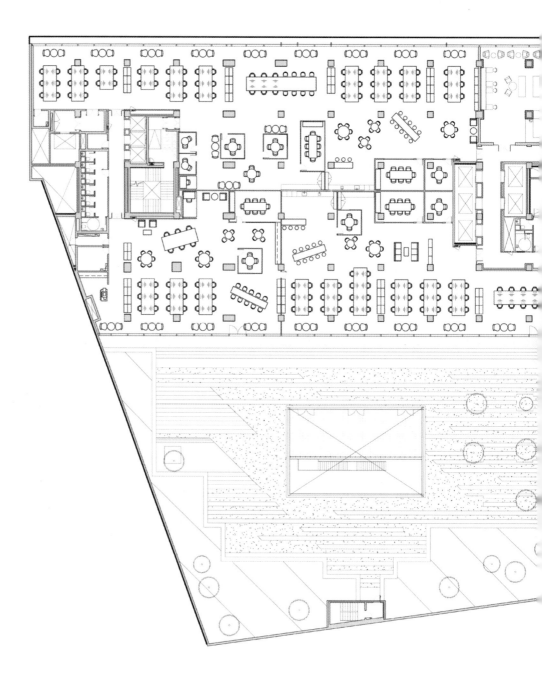

16

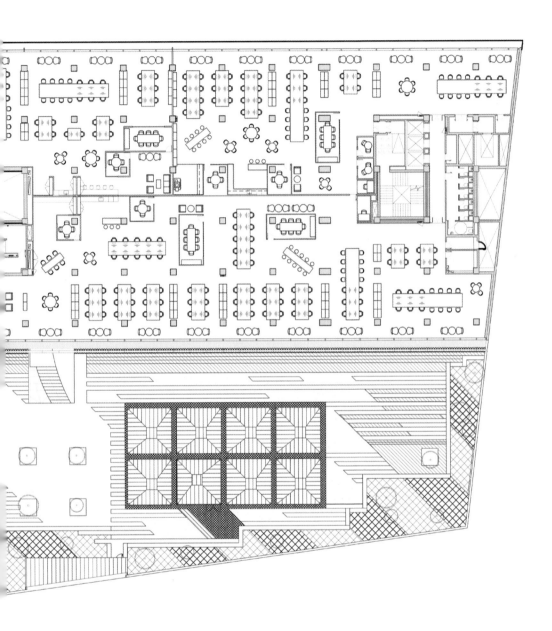

17

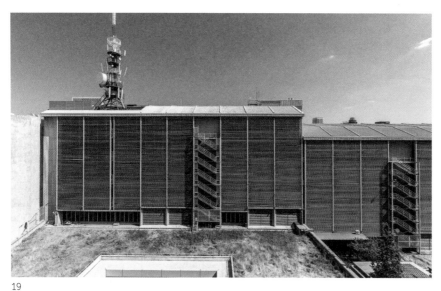

19

The Facts:

Size: 35,000sqm
Location: Madrid
Status: On-site
Year: 2018

Key Features:
26 Rios Rosas has the
largest single floorplate
of any office building in
the centre of Madrid,
at a staggering 7,000sqm,
along with the highest
floor to ceiling heights
at just short of 5 metres
on all levels.

Opinion:
Published,
Building Magazine,
November 2016

16
Typical Stage
3 General
Arrangement
showing office
accommodation.
17
Stage 3
visualisation of
typical workspace.
18
Stage 3
visualisation of
the ground floor
hospitality and
co-working space.
19
Existing South
facing elevation
with solar shading.
20
Stage 3
visualisation of
proposed South
facing elevation
with modern
solar shading and
landscaped terrace.

20

03
London Calling

-

"We live by the river"

London calls loudly. The most dynamic of cities, with an ever-changing skyline that shifts with the constant evolution of modern work. A global hub, it's a place where people come to do business, collaborating on new ideas and making the future real. It stays at the forefront, rethinking how we work and how that's accommodated by the spaces and places we belong in. We no longer go to work; work has become a part of our lives. Just like the city itself, our workplaces must attract workers and give them a reason to be there - because we have the choice to be anywhere. A sense of belonging, a collective identity, the opportunity to do our best work, with the best people. You can find all of that here. London's not just burning with potential, it's on fire.

Just the two of us

—

Preface:

Two successful London-based design agencies merged to form a creative powerhouse with plans for growth. The new space needed to provide a blank canvas for the agency to grow and develop not only its talent, but its own brand and culture.

01
The reception, located at the top of the building and adjacent to client facilities.

02
General arrangement plan of the top floor, including reception.

03
Co-working space adjacent to terrace.

04
A mix of private and semi-private meeting rooms.

05
Research library and touch down space.

01

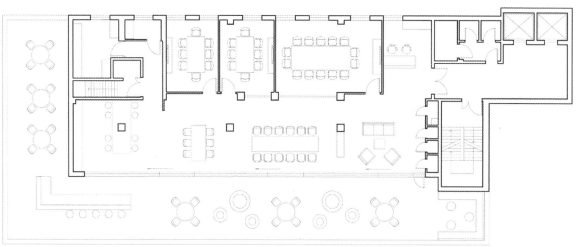

02

03

London is awash with creative possibility. It's always on, never sleeps and perpetually brings people together to form new perspectives and create new opportunities. That's where this story starts.

The building itself is always important, but sometimes the space and what it is designed to achieve takes centre stage. Right here, right now, a new relationship has taken its first major step. An amalgamation, an intertwining, the first days of a new group finding its identity. It needs somewhere to belong to, a place from which to share its collective vision.

A setting with an identity, where being a member is an exclusive privilege, not a chore, is essential.

We need a place to create mischief, explore new possibilities with new people, form and forge relationships and partnerships. We need a space that's malleable enough to let all of this happen, yet defined enough to embrace a single, coherent brand and culture.

This kind of project is all about internal space that unlocks amazing work. Collaboration and connection have to happen, framed by togetherness, to be captured and brought alive in our present and future. The right settings, the right spaces, the right energy.

Welcome home.

04

05

The Facts:

Size:	1,300sqm
Location:	London
Status:	Completed
Year:	2015

Key Features:

Bespoke wall panelling, finishes and ironmongery create a distinctly minimal interior that allows the new brand to grow and develop its character and identity.

Opinion:

-

01

On the farm

—

Preface:
Soho, famous for unmarked doors
that lead to private drinking clubs,
welcomes a new and exceptional
post-production facility on a scale
that can't be found anywhere else
in London.

01
Newly refurbished
Newman Street
facade with
integrated
branding.

02
Reception waiting
area and lobby
artwork/branding.

03
Technical sound/
recording booth.

02

03

When the working day is done, Soho calls those who aren't ready to stop, opening its arms with the promise of adventure. It pulses with hidden opportunity, traditional facades of buildings masking the action behind their doors. Try the handle and in an instant be transported into a dreamland. These are the dens of the minds that never compromise.

In keeping with the area, from the outside this doorway gives away no secrets. At street level, this entrance could lead anywhere. That it could be home to the finest talent in global post-production, housed in a custom-built space that offers everything, is an illusion as enticing as it is deliberate.

How do you create a space for these people, who spend their days and nights creating visual masterpieces? You create possibility – just like they do. Make a space where corridors lead to opportunities, staircases to adventure. Bold, visual, striking in every way, yet nothing is obvious. Each tiny element is designed for a purpose and that purpose is to unleash these people into their adventure of work.

A sophisticated, expansive space, where the most demanding of work is done; this kind of excitement needs to be hidden from view, allowed to do its thing in its own warren before delivering it to the world as a finished article.

100% Soho.

04
Co-working
and hospitality
space adjacent
to external
terrace and
break-out
space.

05
Open/break-out
setting located
among the edit
suites with neon
artwork and
brand features.

06
Support areas
are distributed
throughout the
buildings and
among the
edit suites.

07
Iconic imagery
implemented
as wayfinding
throughout
the building.

08
Interconnecting
stair and
break-out space
between ground
and first floors
connecting
'Hero' edit
suites to
reception and
hospitality
areas.

04   05

06

07

08

09
Interconnecting
stair and break
-out space between
ground and first
floors connecting
'Hero' edit suites
to reception and
hospitality areas.

10
Services were
left exposed
with corridors
for ease of
maintenance.

The Facts:

Size:	3,100sqm
Location:	London
Status:	Completed
Year:	2016

Key Features:
This heavily cellularized
facility of edit suites
is focused on simplicity
of navigation and
integration of support
spaces for guests.

Opinion:
-

09

10

01

Creative platform

—

Preface:

In the beating heart of the city, Kobalt is building the music services platform of tomorrow. As a global company for a bold digital age, it needs a London base that makes the right statement.

01
Area adjacent to
reception/arrival
with hospitality for
clients and visitors.

02
Central corridors
with views to
the Thames.

03

If creativity is currency in the digital age, The River Building offers the ideal location for a team committed to disrupting and changing an industry. Once home to the London Stock Exchange, it resides in the heart of the city, over Cannon Street Station. This place oversees the shift from old to new business as London beats and flows around it.

A platform that enables artists to perform at their peak needs a workplace that empowers.

A place where the creative can mix with the technical, giving rise to collaborations and projects that create the future of the music business. Such a place gives opportunity to everyone, to the unknown and to the superstars, and allows them to thrive in pursuit of a common goal.

This space is focused on real success rather than bravado. Clean, sophisticated lines give way to open spaces, with light as a key feature.

Everything is functional, providing a platform for people. Reflecting the company ethos of honest, simple and humble, the workplace supports everyone in doing the right work, the right way.

Never confused or over-elaborate, it gets out of the way and lets the activity do the talking. It's a synergy that drives success.

Less is more.

03
Arrival
floor and co-
working space.

04
Co-working coffee
bar and event
space.

05
Meeting space and
artist rooms.

06
Touchdown space in
the cafe area.

07
Client and staff
hospitality area.

04

06

05

The Facts:
Size: 3,700sqm
Location: London
Status: Completed
Year: 2018

Key Features:
Open plan space with large
cafe/hospitality area.

Opinion:
–

07

Eastern promise

—

Preface:

In a newly redeveloped corner site in the heart of Clerkenwell Green, The Buckley Building heralded the beginning of a regeneration in EC1 that would see long-neglected buildings brought back to life for West End occupiers looking east for high quality, affordable accommodation.

01

02

01
Rooftop bar and client hospitality space on Level 04.

02
The Buckley Building, with a prominent presence on Clerkenwell Green, was developed by Derwent London.

03-04
Client touchdown
and media space
adjacent to
reception.

05
Secondary
structure
for client
interventions
remains independent
and coordinated
with primary
steel structure.

06
Horizontal
circulation routes
divide open plan
workspace from
the centralized
shared facilities.

04

03

05

The Facts:

Size: 2,180sqm
Location: London
Status: Completed
Year: 2014

Key Features:

Natural materials
and finishes, such
as concrete, oak,
and handmade tiling,
were specified and
detailed to represent
the brand quality.

Opinion:
-

06

07

Clerkenwell has a creative heart and an industrial past. Within striking distance of Silicon Roundabout and the buzz of Shoreditch, it retains a productive elegance as a location where people in the know go to really work. It's the right location for those looking to create substance with style.

As the building came, so did the thinkers, doers, makers and movers. This was a flagship renovation – The Buckley Building used its corner location to grab attention and make waves.

The people it attracts want to do amazing work yet balance it with pleasure, being their best for both themselves and their clients. Curiosity brings them here, opportunity makes them stay.

A space that is at once sympathetic to the area's former industrial age while leading the way into its future. Here, reflected and reborn, a new type of industriousness emerges. Today we brew ideas and interactions between the steel beams and arches.

Caverns and cubbyholes give way to sloping glass vistas. Mosaics and contrasting surfaces challenge inhabitants to create. Bold colours mingle with neutral shades, as corridors stretch into the heartland of possibility. Every area is ready for social productivity, as befits the mood, requirement or style.

This is a calling for people, a challenge to be their best.

07
Handmade tiling within the client facing media space.

08
Layering of finishes and setting out of installations were carefully coordinated to provide a feeling of movement among the primary elements.

09

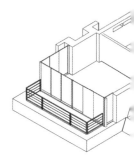

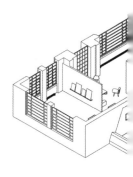

10

09-10
Waiting area and
informal meeting
space within
the atrium.

11
Exploded diagram
showing programme
distribution across
Levels 03 and 04.

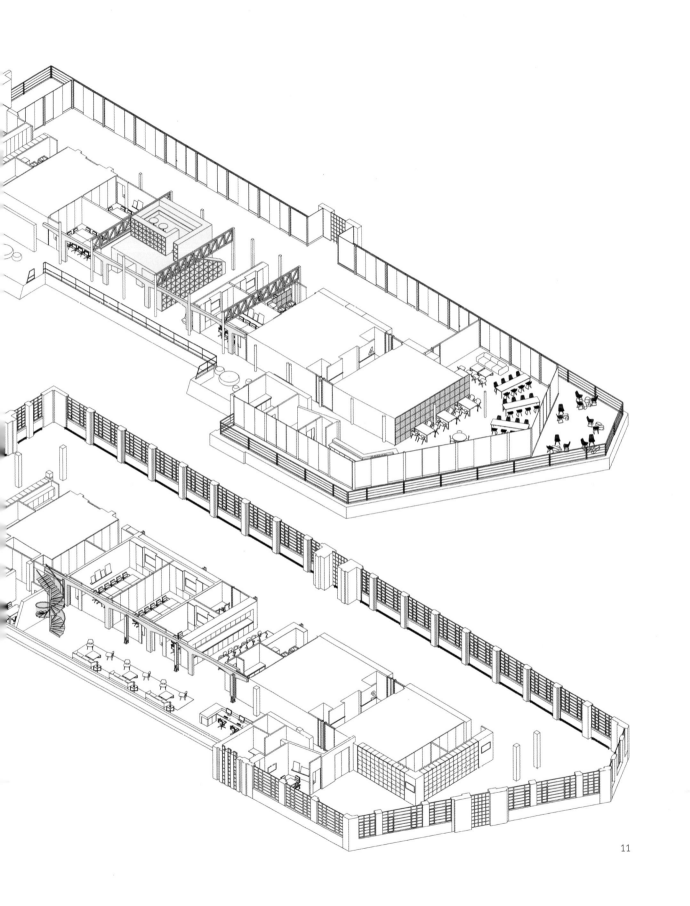

12

13

12
A new mezzanine
level was
introduced to
provide additional
co-working
accommodation
with internal
library space.

13
Client media space,
which also doubles
as hospitality
point for events
when needed.

14

14
The new mezzanine
includes a host
of bookable and
non-bookable
collaborative
spaces.

15-16
The workspace is
a non-hierarchical
agile environment.

15

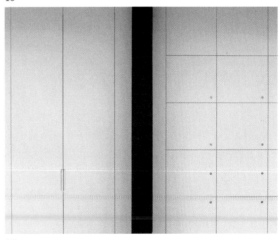

16

01

Alphabeta

—

Preface:
Just off Silicon Roundabout, next door to the Google Campus and within the same neighbourhood as Amazon headquarters, Alphabeta, the home to leading media agency Maxus, is a statement in pared back simplicity and brand integration.

With tech giants as your nearest neighbours, you need personality to find your place in this part of London. Copying is bound to fail; this has to be about you. The ones who make it here are those who are true to themselves.

Maxus knows this and helps its clients navigate the exciting opportunity that the ever-increasing pace of the modern media landscape provides. It's a dynamic leader, focused on its people who, in turn, are focused on leading their clients through a journey.

Creating a workplace that inspires and rewards, helping them forge ahead into the future, in a straightforward way that guarantees success, was the only way to reflect

the company in its workplace. It was an opportunity to redefine space and style for an organisation residing physically and operationally at the juncture between tech and corporate.

A space that offers touches of fun and the unexpected in a setting of energy and refinement. Designed first and foremost for people, this workplace exists for those who work in it. It's a way of releasing them to do their very best work, in engaging, beautiful and occasionally playful surroundings. It's a workplace that flows, plotting a journey into the future.

Bold, beautiful, iconic and individual. Maxus is right at home here.

02

The Facts:

Size:	2,880sqm
Location:	London
Status:	Completed
Year:	2015

Key Features:

Integrated social space
with an interconnecting
stair has become a hub
for both socialising
between staff and
networking with
partners and clients.

Opinion:

Published, Architonic,
November 2016

Published, Architects
Choice, December 2016

Published, Office
Snapshots, December 2016

01
The view for
visitors across
the atrium from
the reception
shows a creative
meeting space.
02
Reception and
waiting area with
branded feature
wall by Spaceman
Studio Ltd.
03
Integrated AV/
media wall
and ceiling
installation for
power distribution
and wayfinding
within reception.

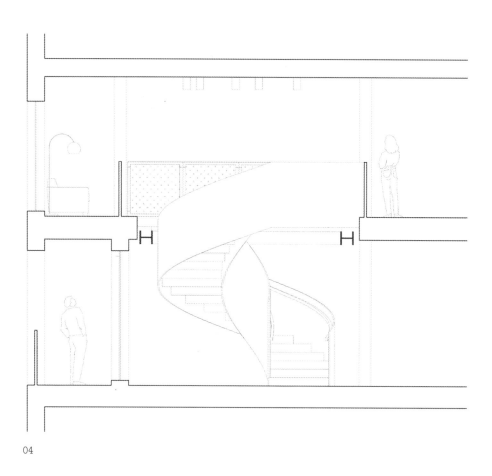

04

05

07

06

04
Concept Stage
section through
the new
interconnecting
spiral stair
between levels.

05-06
Wherever possible
the fabric of the
existing building
is exposed
to contrast
against the
new installations.

07
The spiral stair
and 'bridge' have
been planned to
allow for a more
open double
height space
that can operate
as a 'town hall'
setting for
company meetings.

08

08-09
Open plan
workspace has
been assigned to
multidisciplinary
teams working on
client accounts.

10
Shared co-working
spaces are
distributed around
the floorplates to
allow ease of
communication
and collaborative
working.

11-12
Simple branding
of both rooms and
personal storage
take back seat
to the larger
branding elements
within the space,
all by Spaceman
Studio Ltd.

10

09

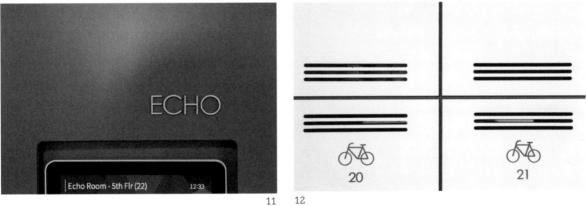

Echo Room - 5th Flr (22)   12:33

20   21

11   12

Open for business

—

Preface:
An invigorating advertising
agency in the heart of London,
with an open and collaborative
culture, is represented in
a series of interventions
that not only helps unlock
creativity, but provides
additional space for growth.

02

01-02
A series of
standalone
installations were
placed within the
existing double
height space
to extend the
variety of
settings available
for co-working
and support
a new agile
working policy.

03
Existing furniture
was re-used and
supplemented
with new where
necessary.

03

Hatton Garden may be an inconspicuous location for the most forward thinking of advertising agencies, but these are people who think differently. Grey London has ambitions that demand doing things in a way that's right for every client, every project, every time. Things are never the same twice.

To achieve such ambition, you need to involve everyone. For Grey, that means opening up the structure of its organisation to remove any trace of hierarchy and ego, recognising that together it is at its most creatively potent, and tearing down the barriers to collaboration and participation.

The resulting challenge was to create a workplace that simultaneously offers a blank canvas and the spark of inspiration for these creative minds to be at their best. Nestled within a building which itself had found reinvention, the stage was set.

Clean lines and curves, streaming daylight and roof vistas provide the basis. Spaces to think, create, collaborate and co-create are found in abundance. Quality finishes make statements without taking centre stage – that's reserved for the people and their ideas. The workplace frames it all.

Grey London operates an open culture and its workplace facilitates and reflects that. An honest space where anything is possible.

Space to think, space to create, space to grow.

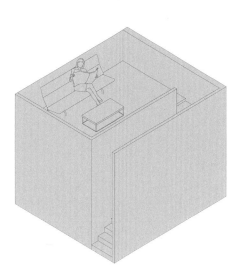
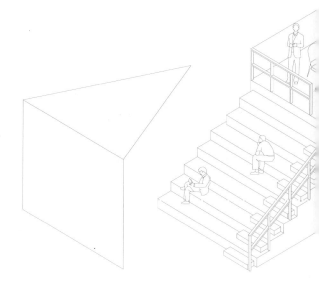

04

04
Developed
design diagrams
illustrating the
three primary
installations
within the existing
workspace.

05
General
Arrangement plans
of all levels with
the Grey office.

06
Two new levels of
co-working space
arranged around
an enclosed
spiral stair.

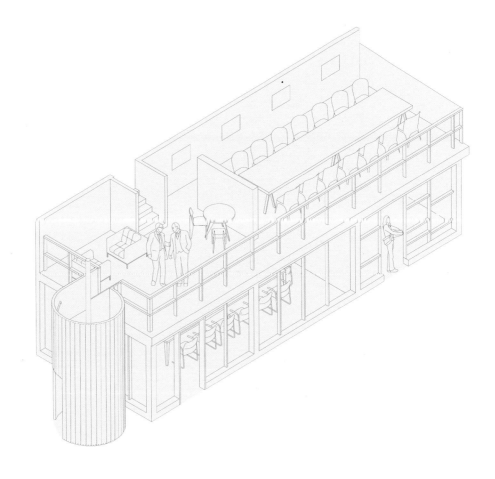

The Facts:

Size:	3,700sqm
Location:	London
Status:	Completed
Year:	2015

Key Features:

The solutions introduced into this existing space not only met the requirements of the agency in terms of providing a variety of work settings, but also added more floor area that is essentially 'rent free' space.

Opinion:

Published, Building Construction Design, August 2015

Published, Architects Datafile, August 2015

Published, Mix Interiors, October 2015

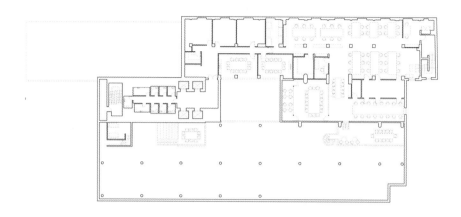

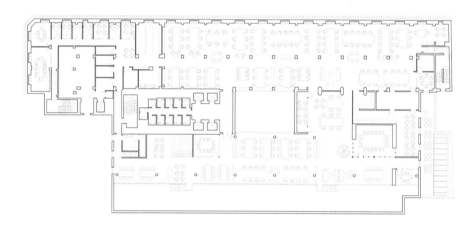

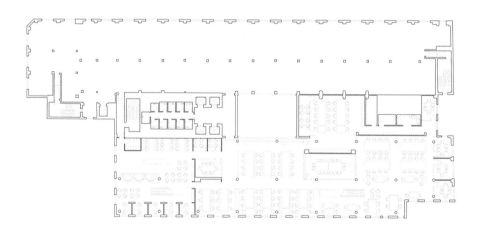

05

The Facts:
Size: 500sqm
Location: London
Status: Completed
Year: 2016

Key Features:
A prominent shopfront
that utilizes the
client's components
to define the space,
a small internal
atrium and an
interconnecting
stair that all feel
integrated into
the showroom and
design studio.

Opinion:
-

01

Look who's talking

—

Preface:
An interactive design studio and showroom in central London has been created to support the international architectural community for global aluminium building systems manufacturer ALUK.

02

03

When your space is your showcase, it's essential to make a statement.

Sleek lines and minimalist finishes that could work in either a domestic or commercial setting are core to its clients' requirements and its London studio needed to reflect that. It was essential to create a location that would make people feel they were at home while they work.

To do this while maintaining a primary focus on ALUK's own products, the space needed to be an enabler. A facilitator of all of these activities, stepping back to throw attention onto the products themselves.

A flowing, stripped back space combines with quality wood and concrete finishes that stay true to the building's fabric, to create the perfect solution. Vibrant splashes of colour, framed by full height internal windows and glanced-through doorways, add touches of excitement and anticipation as the building reveals itself. Function and form combine quietly to create the most effective setting for all uses.

To make a statement, you don't need to shout.

04

06

07

01-02
Arrival at the
ALUK showroom.

03-04
The ground floor
showroom, events
space and informal
meeting room.

05
New inter-connecting
stair located below
the roof lights
towards the rear of
the showroom.

06
New timber
installations add
a warmth to the
core of concrete,
steel and glass of
the base build.

07
Formal meeting room
and presentation
space on the lower
ground floor.

08
Open coffee bar
and small kitchen.

08

Thinking inside the box

—

Preface:
A historic, listed building in Holborn might not be the first thing that comes to mind when thinking of a data analytics marketing business, but this challenging site required a temporary solution that could support co-working.

Making sense of complex streams of historical information from multiple sources before using them to tell a story that solves a problem, is a specific talent. That's exactly what marketing analytics provider Gain Theory (formerly Ohal) does. It's also exactly what it needed us to do for them. Behind traditional, recognisable facades, a building offering the restraints of walls and ceilings needed to be transformed. Functional, useable space was of paramount importance.

The people here like to stay behind the scenes. They see themselves as problem-solving mathematicians and, rather than big, brash statements, they provide functional, informed support. They communicate through the quiet, analytical word in the ear that keeps their clients on track, allowing them to take decisions on the things that make the noise.

To facilitate this in a workplace requires a focus on refined functionality and clear usability. Constrained by the listed status of the building itself, the challenge here was to hold back and create in the most restrained way. A workplace created as an entity within a building, rather than fully integrated as part of its fabric.

By staying true to all of these requirements and stepping back, design allowed the space to emerge. Straight lines, functional minimalist finishes, direct walkways and accessible spaces open up into vistas of the majestic building outside these walls. A place nestled within a place – the perfect reflection of Gain Theory's understated yet important role in its clients' success.

01
Abstract of the stand alone installation within the listed building setting in Central London.
02
The architectural solution effectively acts as a large scale piece of furniture within an enclosed atrium.
03
The historical setting for the new Gain Theory space in London.

02

04   06

05

The Facts:

Size:	500sqm
Location:	London
Status:	Completed
Year:	2014

Key Features:

A minimal, architectural installation arranged over two levels, completely stand alone and offering additional usable floorspace within a previously under utilized internal atrium in a listed building.

Opinion:

–

04-06
A series of abstract photographs that show the new installation in context of the old, as it stands alone within the larger, more open space.

01
The studio, a
non-heirarchical
workspace that
allows staff the
freedom to choose
where to work.

No frills, no fuss

—

Preface:

An under utilized office block in Southwark, surrounded by competition to attract short-term leaseholders within the creative industries, required a cost effective new lease of life ahead of going to market.

The Facts:

Size:	500sqm
Location:	London
Status:	Completed
Year:	2014

Key Features:

The exposed services and structure have been finished to directly contrast with the white walls and natural daylight on to the floors from the large format windows around the perimeter.

Opinion:

-

01

02

05

04

In any area with a reputation for quality, the bar is set high. With local entertainment provided by Shakespeare himself, via The Globe Theatre, and Borough Market showcasing the finest of ingredients and hospitality, this is a truly unique location. In the shadows of the more opulent city buildings, here on the banks of the Thames, the focus is on function without fanfare.

Against a tight budget and short timescale, the right balance was required to attract potential tenants. The Emerson Building needed to be different without being pretentious, attractive while standing back and not taking the limelight away from those within its walls.

Features of the warehouse-style space were maximized to create inviting workplaces, ready to work in, yet simple enough to be personalized. Focusing on light, clean lines and unfussy spaces makes this a place where anyone could work. Reception and common areas offer a refined sense of excitement, fusing comfort and artistic styling, with a nod to both the building's past and its artisan surroundings.

A refined colour palette with high quality finishes allows the space to be punctuated with statement furnishings and artworks. It's inviting, accommodating and feels productive, yet retains an air of understatement.

The Emerson Building, like its neighbour, acknowledges its role as a stage and provides the limelight for others to shine.

03

02-03
Typical CatA office
floors on the
upper levels.

04
Simple and cost
effective fit-out of
all cores and services,
including WCs.

05
Ground floor CatA
office space with steel
columns and original
shopfront retained.

06-07
The reception and
common parts were
given a simple
makeover and brand
identity that would
appeal to the
creative community
within Southwark.

07

06

Start me up

—

Preface:

In 2015, in a building not exactly known as a home for start-ups, Level 09 of The Shard was about to change this pre-conception and this wasn't the only point it had to prove. IO Oil & Gas was also intending to change the way its industry did business.

01

creativity / certainty

powerful thinking

02

Unapologetically striking, The Shard punctuates the London skyline, reaching for the skies. A monument to wealth and high finance, it's a shining beacon - an ecosystem where big business works, eats and sleeps.

Admittedly, not the most likely location for a disruptive start-up. But history shows the only way to mix things up and inject new energy into an established trade is to be in the middle of it.

Bringing a fresh, modern style to an industry renowned for its staid approach, IO Oil & Gas carried bold ambitions to change things for the better. Out with the old and in with the new.

Such a statement needs to pulse through every part of the company. Place creates the platform for people to thrive, so it was essential that IO's space embodied everything it was setting out to do.

Fresh, light colours, natural finishes and exposed services provide an inviting modern contrast to the traditional look and feel expected in the sector. Generous communal spaces and alternative work settings create options for collaboration, flexible working and a personal experience for each individual.

It's a place that offers balance. From The Shard's viewing platform, all of London can be seen: The City to Silicon Roundabout, Soho to the South Bank. Just like IO itself, the space captures and translates all of that into something functional, ambitious and unique.

01
The Shard, the
iconic addition to
the London skyline.

02
The new brand/
concept for IO Oil
& Gas, by H+K
Strategies.

03
Stage 4
general arrangement
plan for Level 09.

04
Stage 2
concept visualisation
for the arrival onto
the floor/reception.

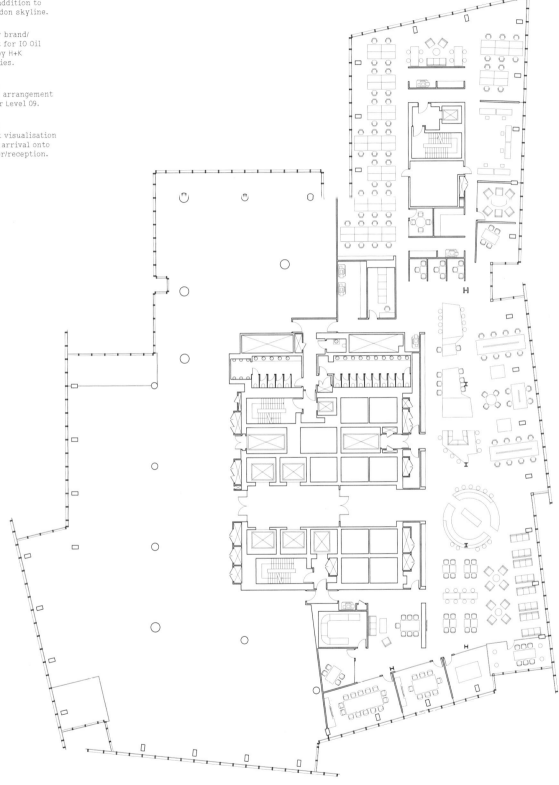

03

The Facts:
Size: 1,400sqm
Location: London
Status: Completed
Year: 2015

Key Features:
The integrated reception,
barista coffee point and
bar is not only a main
feature on arrival into
the space, but also a hub
around which collaboration
and informal meetings
can happen.

Opinion:
-

04

01

Top of the world

—

Preface:

Towering over London from an imposing position, communication leader Finsbury makes a statement in everything it does, so its landmark location needed to convey that sense of quality, expertise and impact.

Effective communication is about using the right medium to impart information. The elite artisans who practice their craft at the highest level need an environment that paints a picture of exquisite quality and finesse.

A global leader trusted by many of the world's most successful companies in strategic messaging needs to make a bold statement. In The Adelphi, an imposing icon of modernist architecture, Finsbury can do just that. The prominent riverside location sets the scene, a direct proclamation that this is the real deal.

An imposing ceiling centrepiece makes the right first impression. The theme of refined quality and exemplary craftsmanship continues throughout.

This is a place where business is done. No nonsense here, the lines and edges speak for themselves, leaving no doubt that this team deals in impact. Exquisite finishing matches wood with classic shades. Detailing shines without being fancy, demanding attention purely through being the best at what it does.

Outside, the world ebbs and flows. Inside, sense is made from all of that chaos. Cutting through the noise with serene clarity is exactly what happens here. No further words are needed.

02

01
Feature ceiling.
02
Corridor leading to
meeting suite.
03
Executive area.

03

05

04

04
View across London
from The Adelphi
Building.
05
Reception area.
06
Detail of feature
ceiling.

The Facts:

Size:	1,200sqm
Location:	London
Status:	Completed
Year:	2017

Key Features:

Open plan executive area, client meeting suite and combination reception/ bar area.

Upfront planning

—

Preface:
An independent, successful, award winning digital agency became part of global powerhouse WPP and transformed to become the London outpost for Possible. It had only nine weeks and limited funds to transform its space for continued success.

01-02
The new reception
and waiting area
for Possible.

01   02

03

At a time of intense change, identity is everything. Observing, understanding and capturing it is what makes things 'Possible'. This group of people had become part of a much larger global family and that newfound collective belonging needed to be reflected in a context of retained individuality.

With a culture that aims to retain a local view of the world at large, and a business approach based around listening, creating and measuring, there is an energy underlying the identity and an intention to unlock the right approaches and the best ideas. Looking on the past as a successful campaign, Possible was gearing to launch into its next one – this time with the world at its feet.

Capturing the essence of the identity that got the team this far, while unleashing it in a new guise, is a challenge. Achieving it came down to staying true to all of it – observing, understanding, capturing, and delivering.

A space for belonging, creating, thinking; somewhere to be inspired. Uncomplicated and direct in its connection with the people who work there, this is a workplace for a successful future. It offers generous communal areas, collaborative spaces to gather and plan, and meeting spaces featuring striking imagery. The Possible workplace doesn't just house its people, it has a constantly flowing conversation with them.

It inspires them to make anything and everything Possible.

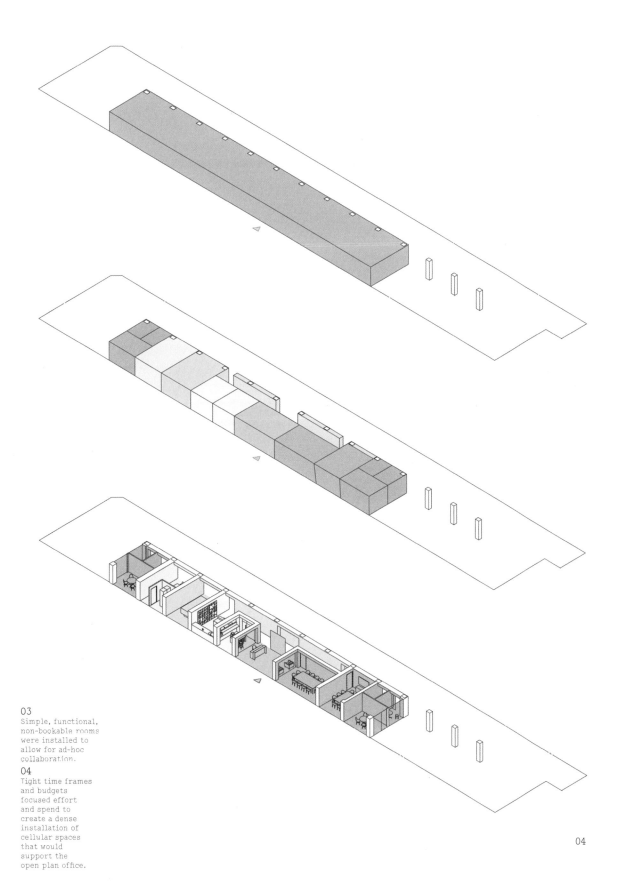

03
Simple, functional,
non-bookable rooms
were installed to
allow for ad-hoc
collaboration.

04
Tight time frames
and budgets
focused effort
and spend to
create a dense
installation of
cellular spaces
that would
support the
open plan office.

04

"It was a wonderful experience working with BDG."

—

Dale Herigstad
Chief Interaction Officer
Possible

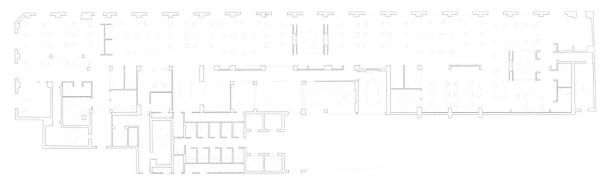

05

06

05
05
General
Arrangement Plan.

06
The Lab was
programmed at
the main arrival
into the space,
so visitors and
clients could
see research
and development
in action.

07
The kitchen and
heart of the agency.

07

The Facts:

Size:	1,100sqm
Location:	London
Status:	Completed
Year:	2012

Key Features:
A simple palette of
finishes and branding
delivered a sophisticated
scheme on a tight budget.

Opinion:
Shortlisted for
FX Awards 2013

Shortlisted for
Mixology 2013

04
Northern Lights
_

No longer the great divide

There was once talk of a north-south divide, but no more. Wherever you look, cutting-edge workplaces are rising. The former industrial heartlands of our northern cities demonstrate that innovation is everywhere. Today, it's possible to draw talent away from the capital, beckoning with lifestyle choices and opportunities to do the best work in the most amazing workplaces. Just because something is outside the spotlight, doesn't make it any less amazing. These are the hidden workplace gems, breathing life into locations and making them great again. Drawing on identity and heritage, they tell an alternative, ongoing story that is helping to define the future of work.

—

(194 - 203)

The docking station

A dockside in Leeds provides the setting for a digital hub that generates content for millions of users worldwide. With plans to house over 700 people across three neighbouring buildings, creative redevelopment of these shell and core sites is key to attracting talent.

(204 - 209)

As simple as XYZ

A city with a long history of breaking the mould, from sport through to music, and fashion to culture. A conceptual co-working environment for a visionary developer in Manchester was designed to redefine and challenge the genre in the city centre.

The docking station

Preface:

A dockside in Leeds provides the setting for a digital hub that generates content for millions of users worldwide. With plans to house over 700 people across three neighbouring buildings, creative redevelopment of these shell and core sites is key to attracting talent.

The Facts:

Size:	6,000sqm
Location:	Leeds
Status:	Completed
Year:	2016

Key Features:

The large glazed facades facing out onto Leeds dock not only offer exceptional daylight to the workspace, but also showcase the innovation and activity within.

Opinion:

Published, Architects Datafile, August 2016

Published, Archilovers, August 2016

Published, MIX Interiors, November 2016

Shorlisted for Mix North Awards 2016

01 Regional Winner – British Council for Offices Innovation Award 2017

A centre for heavy industry, Leeds dock fed commerce, distributing goods into the heart of the city and beyond. Over the years, the noise stopped, the smoke cleared, and the dock became a monument to former glory.

As a renowned pacesetter in creative media, Sky was seeking a Northern technology hub to provide a new home for its development teams. These people work hard, collaborate, create, but they need to think. They also need a beautiful space to belong – somewhere that gives them identity. Three adjacent buildings were redesigned from empty shells. New mezzanine floors were created, with new stair, lift and WC cores added to each building – a complete transformation.

Staying connected to Leeds Dock itself, the design channelled the building fabric, embedding exposed concrete and blockwork into the finish. The most modern of workplaces, embracing the productive industrial heritage of the area it inhabits.

Here, the people are the stars; the building is their platform.

Endeavour has returned to Leeds Dock.

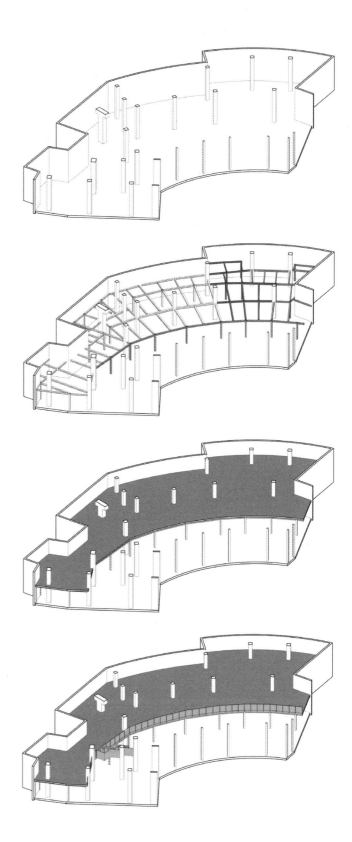

02

01
External
photograph of Sky
Leeds Digital Hub,
by Richard J Wall.

02
Diagram
illustrating
introduction of
mezzanine levels.

03
Work and play
settings are
mixed throughout
the open plan
workspace.

04-07
Structural steel
installations
and new
interconnecting
stairs were
highlighted in
brand colours
throughout the
buildings.

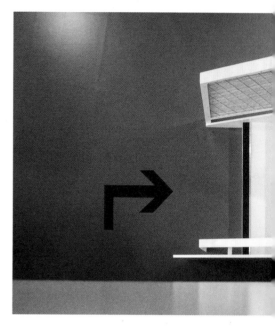

04

06

05

07

" A workspace should be considered a productivity tool, not just a box to store your staff in, and this is exactly what we've got at Sky at Leeds Dock."

—

Matt Grest
Director | Digital Platform Delivery
SKY

09

11

10

08
Shunning the conventions of a standard 'office' fit-out, this environment exposed mostly everything and any coverings were intentionally alternative to the normal.

09–12
Work happens everywhere, planned and un-planned interaction, individual and collaborative working, with no hierarchical structure.

12

01

As simple
as XYZ

—

Preface:

A city with a long history of breaking the mould, from sport through to music, and fashion to culture. A conceptual co-working environment for a visionary developer in Manchester was designed to redefine and challenge the genre in the city centre.

01-06
Competition
visualisations
highlighting
the variety of
co-working/
exhibition spaces
being planned
throughout
the building.

02

03

The Facts:
Size: -
Location: Manchester
Status: Competition
Year: -

Key Features:
A co-working space,
designed to challenge
pre-conceptions
of workspace.

Opinion:
-

04

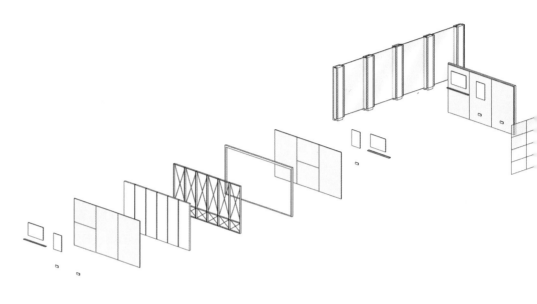

05

06

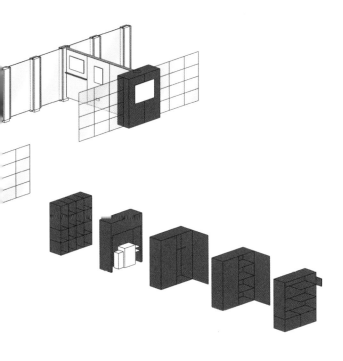

In the beating heart of a bold city, priding itself on leading the way in culture, art and sport, opportunities are forged through determination. As Manchester continues to stake its claim as one of Britain's most progressive cities, media and creative industries are drawn towards its vibrancy.

The XYZ Building rises in the heart of the city. A progressive place for progressive people who need somewhere unique and equally progressive to work.

Developing a concept for a new kind of co-working environment needs to embrace diverse missions, considering the needs of emerging and established businesses alike.

It's a place for people, where work and life flow together to create success. A workplace that forms part of a community.

Collaborative spaces and settings, refined finishes and playful colours combine to create a place to inspire, co-create and work, while enabling workers to retain a sense of individuality. Curved features and dividers form points of interest, breaking the space and encouraging flow.

To be in the space implies effortless simplicity, the hallmark of the city's artists and artisans. Behind it all lies purpose, innovation and hard work.

No fool's gold here.

05
Words
_

"We shape our buildings, thereafter they shape us."

—

Sir Winston Churchill
(1874 - 1965)

01 Strategy

The jump from static to agile organisation is less of a transformation and more of a migration. It is reflective of the culture, behaviours and activities of the organisation, rather than simply its business processes.

The change that does occur adopts a far shallower curve, allowing a focus on the important aspects that relate to supporting what people do, rather than the fundamentals, fears and excitement of wholesale change. Share ratios, a tool once used by many adopting agile working for the first time, just don't feature any more. Second generation agile, which is becoming increasingly evident, has a high degree of clarity, is pragmatic and, even where expectations cannot be met, the element of choice more than makes up for this.

With second generation agile comes a greater maturity of approach to the working environment. The space provides extensive choice, though less frippery (previously seen in slides, swings, fireman poles and the like). The change that agile working has brought has developed and promoted products that are marketeers' dreams, though in reality add little true value to the long term experience. BDG's research recognizes that staff consistently seek out spaces and settings that reflect the diversity between the extremes of group collaboration and individual concentration. These choices are compounded further by the vagaries of personal taste and comfort. Second generation agile looks to tackle these important issues.

Benefits are considerable and evident in the arrangements for architecture, facilities, space and furnishings, being inherent rather than negotiated.

As people realize the benefit of working where it is most appropriate for an activity, and they relish the movement and variety that working in different environments can bring, changing the architecture or furnishings to accommodate more people or different teams is a simple byproduct, rarely a sea change.

The contribution of agile working to the health and wellbeing of staff, although key to BDG's focus on the workplace, is yet to be fully recognized. The next generation is beginning to see that movement and change is a good thing. Neither standing nor sitting is ideal. Transition between workspaces contributes to your health. The location of work settings and space is already becoming part of the wellbeing agenda.

Second generation agile has arrived and we anticipate that this incremental change will be the future of the workplace.

Phil Hutchinson

02 Architecture

—

The average person spends 90,000 hours at work during their lifetime – that's the equivalent of 123 months or 10 years, which makes our work environment as crucial as any of the other spaces we inhabit, whether domestic, educational, public, urban or social.

At BDG, we are interested in the blurring of boundaries between these spaces, a concept that has already taken hold in our everyday lives through mobile technology. Our devices themselves benefit from blurred functionality, and are used for everything from ordering a takeaway on Sunday night to a 20 person video conference on Monday morning. It is these digital devices that are becoming the catalyst for this redefining of physical spaces.

In recent years we have been working on a global architectural strategy for a large multinational company. The strategy is for co-location of a number of 'inner-city' and 'out-post' offices to be housed in one central location and involves the adaptive re-use of big, awkward, 'problematic' buildings.

At the core of this strategy and our conceptual thinking, coupled with a sound economic real estate argument, is a re-imagining of the status of the office or office building in the city. Not as an object or even a building, but as an extension of the public realm. Instead of a rigid, solid boundary from 'public' to 'private' there is a less obvious transition. This thinking has been published under the title *The Ideal Office*.

The Ideal Office research project was a logical progression of trends we had identified in a number of one-off projects as a shift away from conventional office buildings with limited supporting services towards a more 'all-encompassing' environment with facilities and programmes to cover all aspects of daily life, from exercise and wellbeing to catering, laundry and childcare services.

This shift is a further blurring of the public and private lives of the general population, which began with the advent of mobile phones in the 1980s. It has progressed through the digital age via social media, phone apps for domestic chores, online dating, Airbnb and more.

The workplace, previously a private and formal environment, is being eroded and in many organisations workers are given the option of how, where and when they work. This evolved form of flexible working allows opportunities for a more open building programme. Our hypothesis for this part of the project, and the subject of our continued study and analysis, is as follows:

'The traditionally private office environment is becoming more akin to the public realm in large city centres – coffee shops, hairdressers, gyms and bars are now commonplace in large commercial buildings – in a time of public spending cuts and stagnating wages these resources could be of benefit to the general population.' Or – 'how can private commercial building benefit the urban population?'

Toby Neilson

03 Scared of Change

▬

Change is a scary word. It means things aren't staying the same.

Traditionally, we see change as a move from A to B, with the aim being to get from one to the other. In our workplaces, we tell the people what is happening and why, training them as necessary. But we need to do more!

Workplace change can affect our people, their working environment and the way they work. Its effects are experienced on a personal level. Every change project is part of a wider organisational evolution. We need to keep this bigger picture in mind when addressing transition and transformation, so we can connect people with their work and workplace - not just tell them what we expect to happen.

The success of any change rests on creating a genuine connection between people and the transition. Fail to create that connection and the change project is at best likely to fall short, at worst fail. Most sources agree that around two-thirds of change projects fail to meet their objectives, which means that most traditional change management approaches are missing the mark somewhere.

As humans, we connect with our work and workplace in very specific ways, individually and collectively.

Change alters that connection. Dealing with it requires space and exploration.

To avoid productivity and morale dips, while harnessing the benefits of an investment in change, it needs to be approached more creatively - in a more human way. Connect people directly with change; don't just tell them about it!

Successful change management comes from so many places. It's an adaptive, context-specific thing, not something that can be taught as a procedure. Look on change as a transition - helping people to move from one set of circumstances to another.

Successful transition management is a combination of psychology, creativity, communication, exploration and anything else that may be appropriate to creating that effective connection between people and change. It should always come from a positive place and support those affected to examine, understand, imagine and own the transition.

Wherever change happens, there will always be some trepidation, even where people know the outcomes will be positive. Maximize the benefits and minimize the pitfalls with a carefully planned transition programme, just for your organisation.

Andy Swann

04 Management of Me

Advances in mobile technology and an emphasis on knowledge sharing mean boundaries between work and life are blurring at an ever-increasing rate - so much so that the very term 'going to work' is being redefined.

And, as work encroaches on our every waking hour, our personal life increasingly pervades the workplace. The 'Management of Me' in what we once knew as the working week is now organized in a parallel universe of online social communication, be that with old friends, work colleagues or even clients.

Facebook's Chief Operating Officer Sheryl Sandberg highlights this in her book *Lean In*, and sees it as a change for the better: "I am now a true believer in bringing our whole selves to work. I no longer think people have a professional self for Mondays through Fridays and a real self for the rest of the time. That type of separation probably never existed and, in today's era of individual expression, where people constantly update their Facebook status and tweet their every move, it makes even less sense."

Dr Carsten Sørensen at the London School of Economics is an expert on the relationship between technology and behaviour in the workplace. His findings back up Sandberg's view: "We are entering the century of the individual. This is the century of me, me, me, and the notion that you have the right to express yourself as an individual. That will soon be the hallmark of any organisation."

While employees' behaviour at work has come to include more of their online social persona, employers are still working out how to respond. Judith Heerwagen, Kevin Kelly and Kevin Kampschroer see these changes as a new psychological contract between employers and employees. In their paper,

The Changing Nature of Organizations, Work and Workplace for the National Institute of Building Sciences in Washington DC, they say the old contract was "all about job security and steady advancement within the firm". In contrast, "the informal, 'psychological contract' between workers and employers - what each expects of the other - focuses on competency development, continuous training, and work/life balance."

But how will this shift affect the corporate brand? How do you keep staff on message, walking the walk, when they are engaged - either physically out of the office or on-screen - elsewhere? In the old days, a good dose of internal communications would set everyone straight, but that's no longer the case.

One upshot will be an office environment that must better reflect the priorities of these individualistic individuals. Phil Hutchinson of BDG architecture + design points out that in practical terms, people want their personal space to be as mobile as their technology. "People still want their own space and to personalize it. But they also want the flexibility to work wherever they want. So personalisation tends to go with them. Traditionally, it was a family photo on the desk. Nowadays, people take their very personal branding with them, so they have same screen drop as they take it with them on their iPads."

And, in broader brand terms, as employees allow their individualism to encroach on their working selves, employers must figure out how best to accommodate - and possibly even to encourage - the Management of Me. Because as the world becomes more individualistic, it will be businesses that foster such a mindset within a productive work environment that will come out on top.

Clare Dowdy

05 Green Workplace

The environmentally friendly workspace has reached a critical mass. There are now many ways to rate how eco-friendly an office is. The UK headquartered BREEAM alone has certified in excess of 40 million square metres of floor area since 1990, while the likes of LEED, which is part of the US Green Building Council, promises so much to buildings going through its green standard, such as lower operating costs, increased asset values and tax rebates. Offering a green solution no longer works as a differentiator, it is now expected and a given. Surely this message has been thoroughly driven home to developers and landlords by now that tenants want green buildings?

Not across the board, argues Clive Hall, director with BDG architecture + design, who looks after sustainability. "Quite a few of the larger spec offices and particularly those I'd describe as landmark schemes have solid green credentials. It depends on the developer of course but some recognize going green as a marketing opportunity." While we may be living in much more positive economic times than we were five years ago, in terms of rents and yields, any competitive edge, such as a green rating, could prove crucial in the next 12 months and beyond.

A useful indicator of the current demand for sustainable office design is to look at the supplier side, where, it seems, we're not stuck but moving forward with positive signs abounding. From flooring to task chairs, suppliers are launching new products specifically with environmental ratings in mind and investing in manufacturing to make it even more green.

The green message hasn't got through to all developers, however, as Hall continues. "Moving further down in size, there will be the type of developments that tick all the boxes in terms of current regulations, such as Part L, but probably won't offer things like grey water recycling. We have been working on a couple of developments recently where the shell and core the developer specified will probably go through the BREEAM process but I wouldn't necessarily say they are green buildings."

As well as BREEAM and LEED, there is also the Ska rating. Instead of assessing the environmental impact of whole buildings, Ska is an environmental assessment method, benchmark and standard for non-domestic fit-outs, led and owned by the Royal Institution of Chartered Surveyors (RICS). Advocates of the Ska rating point to the fact that it helps organisations from landlords, developers, consultants, fit-out contractors, members of the supply chain as well as occupiers, to make informed decisions about fit-out projects. This is particularly crucial given the growing importance of sustainability on the corporate agenda, and the various pieces of legislation that relate to green matters.

However, the sheer proliferation of different rating systems is still proving difficult for some end users: "We do see a lot of clients who know the basics about what BREEAM or LEED mean but they come to us and admit it's a bit of a minefield for them and so they look to us to give them some advice," Hall says. Thankfully, some end users don't just want to work in a green office because it's a great marketing message or is going to save them money. "They do it because it's the right thing to do, and with our passion for sustainability, we can definitely help."

Helen Parton

06 Global vs Local

When video-conferencing technologies first hit the market seven years ago, many predicted a decrease in business travel and a severe impact on the way we work. The main pitch, after all, was that these technologies could simulate face-to-face interaction and therefore eliminate the need to (and cost of) travel. Yet recent surveys show that business travel in Europe and America is increasing annually despite the recession and remote working. So why do humans still seek face-to-face communication in the world of work? And could this be about to change?

Humans have a deep-seated need for communication. In essence, communication technology is an extension of the desire that drives us to meet in person. The issue, however, is that while IT-based communication was heralded to improve and speed up working processes, it is increasingly found to have an adverse effect. In a recent book, *Business Reimagined*, the established thought leader and former Chief Envisioning Officer at Microsoft UK, Dave Coplin, examines why the way we use technology at work is actually becoming counterproductive: "We spend our working days [...] batting communication [emails] back and forward in a sort of nightmarish game of digital ping-pong." Coplin feels the risk is that people are focused on the processes rather than the outcome, which slows down decision making. This could be one reason why many people feel a face-to-face meeting cuts to the chase.

Gill Parker, CEO at BDG, has also experienced a rise in inefficiency due to technological habits: "I feel the amount of face-to-face meetings has stayed much the same, but the in-between conversations via email, video or audio call have multiplied. Senior staff members are expected to listen into conference calls, often leading to less focused and concise communication, because people concentrate more on covering themselves." This is exactly where Simon Phillips, IT Director at Brand Union, sees the problem. The fact that email is traceable means that people ponder and act more cautiously than they would in person. They are less spontaneous, disabling a natural flow of conversation. But Phillips believes this is all about to change: "There are new products emerging that offer the best of both worlds. So-called unified communication systems allow instant and spontaneous use of all IT-based communication tools at the same time."

Phillips gives the example of how, with video-conferencing, booking the room or the logistics of who is available when often ends up being a journey in itself. "With a unified comms system you can always see who is online and available, then instant message that person, transfer between audio or video call, all from your desktop. You can invite others to join spontaneously, look at files together right there and then rather than 'send a PDF later'. There are multiple options, and the feedback we have received so far is that people really like how it has made their work communication faster, easier and most importantly more intuitive."

Could this mean that technological communication might alter our instincts and become second nature? Jeremy Myerson, who holds the Helen Hamlyn Chair of Design at the Royal College of Art in London, is convinced that, even if conferencing technologies become ubiquitous and achieve real-time, high-definition quality, they will never substitute for the need to interact in person: "As an example, I'm currently editing a book and have been corresponding with my co-author via email, Skype, Dropbox etc., but we never got more done than when we met up in person for three hours over a coffee."

In today's world, our ways of communicating have become more and more complex; each method, whether email, text, phone or video call, serves a different purpose. Maybe combining all of these forms of communication can, over time, become as instinctive as a personal conversation. But technology will always remain a facilitator, not a substitute. Travel and face-to-face meetings will never die out. In much the same way, the office has evolved to become a social hub, responding to predictions of its doom by highlighting the enduring need to socialize. While technology might make the world a smaller, better-connected place, it can't eradicate the difference between a Facebook friend and a real friend – nothing can ever replace looking someone in the eye and shaking their hand.

Kerstin Zumstein

07 Trust & Transparency

—

Over 10 years ago, BDG designed a feature stand for an inaugural workplace exhibition. The stand was designed to provoke thought and discussion around the themes of 'trust' and 'alienation' in the workplace. As workplace designers, we were facing both as challenges to developing new ways of working. Now, more than a decade later, new ways of working have evolved significantly, and gathered a multitude of new names and descriptors along the way, but the core issues that all management teams have to deal with to create real change in their organisation remain the same - trust and alienation. Grant Gibson's column below argues that it's not just management style that influences trust, but that both interior and exterior design can also play a part. It's about balance in all things - too much transparency can be as devastating as too little.

Several years ago, I wrote a piece for an architecture magazine where I celebrated the 10th anniversary of the Stirling Prize for architects by spending a week travelling around the country to previous winners and seeing how they stacked up. It was a fascinating trip charting a brief moment in British history of (often) lottery-funded architectural splurging. The perfectly decent but hardly iconic Centenary Building by Stephen Hodder for the University of Salford won in the Prize's first year for instance, but by 2004 the gong had gone to the Foster and Partner's designed 30 St Mary Axe, better known, of course, as The Gherkin. Along the way there were surprises: magnificent though the old steel works are, should Wilkinson Eyre's Magna Centre in Rotherham really have beaten The Eden Centre to the prize in 2001? And there were flaws: on a sunny day it's impossible to sit in the front few rows of the Lord's Media Centre without being fried as the sunshine pours through the unshaded window.

Notions of lightness and transparency had cropped up in a number of the buildings I'd visited - from Fosters' American Air Museum at Duxford to Will Alsop's new take on the traditional library in Peckham - none more so than the celebrated Laban Centre in Deptford, designed by Herzog & de Meuron. In many respects there's nothing wrong with the thinking behind this. By its nature, transparency is more democratic. The idea of Laban's design was that the dancers and administrators could see and be seen all around the building, rather than being hidden away in separate studios or offices. This meant in turn that communication would improve, ideas could be shared and hierarchy flattened. Only I wasn't convinced. As I wandered around on my tour, I noticed that my presence was having a surprisingly disruptive effect. As anyone who has ever done amateur dramatics will testify, the rehearsal period is an intensely private time, where experimentation takes place, relationships are forged and mistakes are made. However, the building's design neglected this, exposing the dancers when they were at their most vulnerable. I was intruding.

It left me with a deep mistrust of this drive for transparency that is currently so common in the contemporary workplace. In the same way that out of town supermarkets destroyed the corner shop before repopulating the same sites with their own 'Metro' style versions, so management and designers have conspired to rip out cellular offices by going open plan only to create new pieces of furniture that provide employees with the sense of privacy they once took for granted. Over the years, breaking down the walls of the office has been made to sound like an egalitarian act when it is nothing of the sort. Having the company's executives sit among their staff is, at its most basic level, supposed to prove they are all in the same boat, but the effect is usually illusory. Suffice to say that, since it became prevalent, social mobility in Britain has dropped and the gap between the rich and poor has widened to an unbridgeable chasm. Instead, all too often, it's about tightening control rather than promoting creativity. Having been involved in a couple of office re-designs during my career, it seems to me opening the floor plan has the effect of inhibiting, like at Laban, rather than freeing the staff.

Technology plays its part too. I am happy to accept that in some jobs the shared diary is necessary for safety reasons, however, it can also be used to keep a tighter rein on employees. That's one of the reasons I still carry an old fashioned paper version around with me.

It seems to me that trust is the most empowering emotion in the workplace. Once you feel trusted by your manager and colleagues, you are more likely to be more productive, to freely volunteer to put in longer hours, and to enjoy the job you do. However, many of office design's innovations are based around the economics of fitting more people into less space, and a more subtle form of Taylorism, dressed up as something altogether more democratic. They are the proverbial wolf in sheep's clothing, inspired by the desire to control, rather than to promote trust.

Grant Gibson

08 Dissolving Boundaries
—

One of my favourite installations at a recent London Design Festival was the Simplified Beauty show at SCP. It was seeing the display of traditional ceramics from Mashiko that made me realize how much British design has changed and matured since I started writing about it 20 years ago. Back then, Sheridan Coakley's store was the bastion of cutting-edge British design. It was Coakley who promoted the likes of Jasper Morrison, Terence Woodgate, Matthew Hilton, (the sadly late) James Irvine and Michael Marriott to an often ambivalent British public. In the mid-90s design was tribal; you were either part of the nascent Shoreditch scene or a cushion scatterer from Chelsea Harbour; companies were either modern and innovative and exhibited at 100% Design or traditional and conservative, in which case their natural environment was at Decorex, held in the leafy, suburban environs of Syon Park. Some of us on the side of progress genuinely believed we were contributing to a profound change in British culture, that with the likes of Blur and Blair we could somehow re-invent the nation in our own image.

However, nearly 20 years on, it seems we've all learned to relax; the tribes are (slowly) converging. Pluralism reigns. Over the past few years, SCP has exhibited at Decorex, for instance, alongside contemporary companies such as Pinch, Aram and Eley Kishimoto, which would have been nigh on inconceivable even a decade ago. And there's been no more obvious signifier of this change than the re-emergence of craft and the fetishisation of the handmade. Not so long ago, craft came with largely negative connotations of a forgotten England. How things have changed! From being a dirty word, it has almost become a badge of honour. I edited the designjunction catalogue this year and it was fascinating to see how many exhibitors were desperate to emphasize their craft credentials. In an interview I did with Alberto Alessi, for example, he described his vision of the company as: "A combination of fine craftsmanship and advanced design research, following the model of Wiener Werkstaette at the beginning of the twentieth century but rooted in contemporaneity." Suddenly craft, craftsmanship and the handmade are seen as having cultural and (probably more importantly) commercial cachet.

So why has this happened? Well, the fact of the matter is that the 'make-do-and-mend' end of the craft spectrum traditionally tends to thrive in times of economic strife, when people need to find ways of making their stuff go further. This has been compounded by the burgeoning inequalities of British society, in which the super-rich have become richer, meaning the luxury end of the market, which has always traded on hand making, has continued to prosper. Nearly 15 years after Naomi Klein published *No Logo* it also seems that a strata of consumers (middle class and affluent) are paying more attention to how and where their goods are made, aping a recent trend in the food market. In the same way that some shoppers like to know that their chicken breasts are organic, corn-fed or farm-assured, so products that haven't been made under exploitative conditions have found a receptive audience.

It's fair to say that the ambitions of many of the best young designers have changed too. Whereas the ultimate aim was once to get spotted by a major (often Italian) manufacturer and create industrially made products for the mass market, now many of the most interesting graduates are more intent on doing projects that critique consumerism and shy away from globalisation. Allied to this is the fact that many of those same (often Italian) manufacturers have become increasingly risk-averse during the recession, and rely on a small pool of globally renowned designers. Meanwhile, technology has allowed micro-manufacturing to flourish and social media means that makers can now find a potentially huge market.

Arguably this means that the relationship between design, manufacturing, and craft is more tightly knit than at any time since the Industrial Revolution. The perceived boundaries between craft and design are being broken.

Grant Gibson

06
Credits

_

"We are a team of
architects, designers
and creative thinkers."

—

Client list 2012 - 2018

▬

Aberdeen Asset Management	Grafton Advisors
Added Value	Great Portland Estates
Addison Group	Grey
AKQA	GroupM
Aldgate Developments	GroupM Entertainment
ALUK	GSK
Balfour Beatty	GVA
Blast Radius	Handelsbanken
Blue Hive	Hearst Magazines
BNY Mellon	Heath Wallace
Bruce Shaw	Helen Bamber Foundation
BT	Hill & Knowlton Strategies
Coley Porter Bell	Hogarth
Dairy Crest	IHS Markit
DfID	Insight Investment
Digit	Investec
Ecclesiastical Insurance Group	IO Oil & Gas
EDF Energy	J. Walter Thompson
ELLE	JLL
Essence	Kantar
Farebrother	Kinetic
Finsbury	Kobalt
Forward Group	LendLease
Future Designs	LFEPA
Future Learn	Lightspeed Research
Gartner	London Borough of Brent
GE Capital	Match.com
Geometry	Maxus

MEC
Mentor Graphics
Millward Brown
Mindshare
Ministry of Justice
MoneySuperMarket
Montagu Evans
Ogilvy & Mather
Ogilvy Group
Ogilvy Healthworld
Ogilvy One
Ogilvy PR
Ogilvy Primary Contact
Ohal Group
Oracle
Oxford Properties
Paragon
Pershing
Pfizer
Possible
PricewaterhouseCoopers
Quintiles
Rostelecom
Royal London Group
Safra
Scholz & Friends
Scottish Widows
Seadrill Management

Sky
Southwark Council
St John Ambulance
Standard Life Investments
Sudler & Hennessey
Superunion
Teach First
The Brand Union
The Exchange Lab
The Farm Group
The Treehouse
TNS
Turner & Townsend
USM
VML
Wates Group
Wavemaker
Whitbread
WPP
WTMS
Wunderman

Partners list 2012 - 2018

▬

8 Build	Coleman Bennett International
967 Arch	Colliers International
ABG	Collins Construction
Acrylicize	Como
Adnitt Acoustics	Complete Moves
Aecom	Cordless Consultants
Alinea	Cube Interior Solutions
AMS Ltd	Cundall
Appleyard & Trew	Cushman & Wakefield
Arup	Dorrington
Axa Real Estate	DWI
b720	EC Harris
Barry Jobson Architects	Edward Charles & Partners
Becken Development	Edward Symmons & Partners
Bedford & Bedford	Emmaus Consulting
Blue Sapphire Consultancy	Farebrother
BNP Paribas	Flatt Consulting
Bollingbrook LLP	Forbes Consulting
Boon Godbold	Fothergill
Bruce Shaw	Frankham Consultancy
Burke Hunter Adams	Fraser CRE
Buro Four	Gardiner & Theobald
Buro Happold	Gareth Gardner Photography
Butler & Young	GDM
BW Interiors	Gerald Eve
CB Richard Ellis	Gleeds
Chapman BDSP	GPDE
Cluttons	Grontmij

Gryphon Property Partners
GVA
Hall Kemp
Hilson Moran
Hoare Lea
Hunter Acoustics
Hurley Palmer Flatt
Hurst Peirce + Malcolm
Instant Group
Interserve Construction
Invigour Ltd
ISG
Jackson Coles
Jackson Rowe
James Andrew International
Jefferson Smith Photography
JLL
Johnson Controls
Kier South Western
Knight Frank
Leslie Clark
London Fit Out
M&G Real Estate
Mace
Manual Creative
Matheson Whiteley
Medland Metropolis
Milk

Mishcon de Reya LLP
Mix Consultancy
MLM
Out of the Blue
Overbury
Paragon
Parkeray
Qatari Diar
Quantem
Randall Simmonds
Red Engineering Design
RIO
RSP
Savills
Spaceman Studio
Stanway Interiors
Structure Tone
Sweett Group
Telereal Trillium
Temple Bright
The Furniture Practice
Troup Bywaters + Anders
Turner & Townsend
Waterman Group
Wates Group

BDG is a team of architects,
designers and creative thinkers.

They are listeners and
communicators, collaborators
and solution seekers.

BDG believes that architecture is
most successful when it is able to
connect to people and spaces.

Their role is to help make those
connections. That's why they focus
on finding the unique solution for
each client.

Every transformation has a story,
individual to the business, their
people and their space.